Thinking Like A Start-Up

Building & Managing Internet Ventures

Dan Gudema

Copyright © 2014 Dan Gudema

All rights reserved.

ISBN-10: 1502735032
ISBN-13: 978-1502735034

DEDICATION

This book is dedicated to my wife Linda, my sons Victor and Max, my mother Madeline, father Norman, sister Michelle, brother Jonathan and to all the friends, business associates and people who put up with me talking and talking and talking about tech start-ups, venture deals, mergers, acquisitions, and public shells without ever being the real deal.

CONTENTS

Acknowledgments	I

START-UPS

Starting-Up	1
5 Critical Must Answer Questions For Start-ups	Pg 16
Start-up Web Business Models	Pg 22
10 Start-up Web Business Ideas	Pg 30
Tech Mind vs. Business Mind	Pg 38
Learning To Fail Fast The Hard Way	Pg 44

START-UP MARKETING

Web Branding	Pg 52
How To Write A Strategic Marketing Plan	Pg 58
Insecure Focused vs. Secure Focused	Pg 78
Our Decreasing Need To Remember Anything	Pg 84

WEB PRODUCT MANAGEMENT

Digital Feature Discovery	Pg 96

Pivot: How To Avoid The Big Disaster — Pg 118

Feature Overload in Web Product Management — Pg 126

ABOUT PEOPLE

How To Responding To New Ideas — Pg 134

Managing The IT Person — Pg 140

Learning Is Earning — Pg 146

On Leadership — Pg 152

Don't Be Ordinary — Pg 158

Clean Your Team From The Top Down — Pg 164

WEB TECH

The New Web Technology World Order — Pg 172

Passwords, Security, Tech Snafu's & Support Tech — Pg 178

Web Migrations And Taking Sites Live! — Pg 186

The End Of Cable TV As We Used To Know It — Pg 192

On Words: Web Linguistics — Pg 198

A Few Final Words — Pg 207

Thinking Like A Start-Up

ACKNOWLEDGMENTS

I wanted to acknowledge the following people who have impacted me with their thoughts as either a mentor, friend, associate, a client, a customer or through their written word: Terry Aaronson, Roy Abrams, Scott Adams, Zee Aganovic, Carlos Arenas, Jonah Berger, Alex Barenboim, David Barnett, Jay Ravi Behara, Berkowitz, Jeff Bezos, Jonathan Bomser, Dennis Boyle, Ken Brink, Ben Chodor, Michael Clarke, Charlie Corsello, Andre Cvijovic, S Turn Dean, Michael De Biase, Metin Dimirci, Bernie Dohrmann, David Drake, Shomari Drew, Jim Dygert, Meredith Epstein, Mark Ernst, Brad Feld, Brian Fisher, Lillian Fisher, Robert Fletcher, Tom Flynn, Howard Fluker, Alex Funkhouser, Alex Furmansky, Francis Fytton, Vince Gelormine, Malcolm Gladwell, Jim Goldfarb, Jahyun Goo, Anthony Gore, Matt Gore, Keith Gore, Kim Graham, Jason Greenwald, Mark Griggs, David Green, Guillermo Grossen, Mike Haldas, Richard Harvey, Robert Hays, Elliot Harris, Taylor Hazelhurst, Craig Henderson, Andy Hill, Zach Hoffman, Carlos Holtzer, Mary Holtzer, Tony Hsieh, Derek Huang, Bryant Ibana, Thomas Jaffee, Elias Janetis, Josh Joffee, Adam Judah, Michael Kahlowsky, Gary Kahn, Brian Katz, John Kemp, Anthony Kennedy, Young Kim, Andy Klepner, Adam Kravitz, Steve Krug, Mark Laymon, Mitch Lefkofsky, Guy Kawasaki, Robert Hayes, Mitch Lasky, Anthony Lew, Fawad Malik, Lee Magnus, William McDaniel, Shabnam Memarbashi, Sramana Mitra, Gabe Hall, Michelle Marr, Myron Marlin, Franc Nemanic, Mark Neppl, Brad Nickels, Bob Norville, Steve Nudelberg, Brian Nunez, Dhruv Patel, Wil Padron, Jansen Pennock, Liam Pender, Andy Pittaluga, Gary Plitchka, Marcia Pounds, Alvaro Quesada, Andrew Rachmell, Andrew Rudnick, Matt Trask, David Ralph, Cass Riese, Sundrea Ryan, Maeda San, Jordan Serlin, Tom Scott, Dimitry Shaposhnikov, Kevin Sheward, Alan Shimel, Bobby Schwartz, Jeff Schwartz, Alan Stahler, Mark Star, Zackary Stein, Eric Strauss, David Sumka, Lia Sweeney, Matt Tabin, Raleigh Trecha, Andy Turner, David Tyreman, Lane Vance, Larry Van Dusseldorp, Dan Verkman, Darren Wadholtz, Dennis Wakabayashi, Marc Wigder, CJ Wilson, Jared Wolf, Hidetoshi Yagi, Toshi Yamasaki, Arturo Zamora

The trend is a train. You see the train coming down the track; or you see it passing you by; or the train is gone and you are running after it!

Dan Gudema

Start-Ups

If you are at the concept stage for your start-up, keep your wits about you. Listen to others and learn, but only do what you think is best.

STARTING-UP

Why do you need to think like a start-up?

Because it just makes sense! It does not matter if you work at the biggest company in the world or you have a concept for a start-up. They all run into the same process of figuring out how or what a site or mobile app is going to do and how to make revenue and survive. This book is called "Thinking Like A Start-Up" because Internet tech start-ups at the concept stage need to think like a start-up and not a big corporation. Trust me, it's easy to not think like a start-up if you have spent your entire career working for a big company. If you are working for a big corporation that is coming up with a new Internet service or mobile apps you still need to be figuring out how to get it done. You still have to think like a start-up to be successful! When meeting with clients and start-ups I ask an even more important question. How can you make money right now related to your concept?

Let's back up a second. Who is this book for and why are you reading it?

If you are remotely interested in starting or own an Internet venture. If you work for a small to large corporation and are in IT, online marketing or have a general interest in the web, you will get a lot out of this book. If you have no interest in how the web works or how to build a successful web business, website, mobile app or other tech tool, you still will get something out this book, especially if you are trying to understand how tech start-ups function. Thinking Like A Start-Up covers a variety of topics from figuring out what start-up businesses work to Digital Feature Discovery, online marketing and thoughts on a bunch of web related stuff. If along the way, this books helps you create a start-up or improve upon an existing site and get more value in the form of revenue, building and selling an asset or changing the world that is terrific!

How Is This Book Different?

This book is not a how-to guide to building start-ups. There are already 100 books out there like that. There are a few I highly recommend reading. I even mention them in this book. This book is about the thought process that I went through as I worked with tech start-ups and worked on my own tech start-up. These are small vignettes that I put together which try to make you think a little. It covers a lot of IT issues and product management issues I have faced while working at big corporations. It is about fundamental thinking in building out your start-up or web service.

From 2009-2014 I wrote a series of blog articles about start-ups, websites, mobile apps and a few other things along the way. These thoughts and philosophies reflect my work as a consultant, developer and seller of social networks, dating sites, mobile apps and a variety of tech start-ups. Personal conversations with partners, clients, mentors and tech start-up founders over the years have given me the inspiration for everything you read here.

A Diamond In The Rough

Every once while networking or talking with customers, partners or friends I would run into an important concept that I just wanted to write about. Initially it all ended up in my blog. http://www.strategicpoints.com/blog/. I have to acknowledge that almost all these blog entries and concepts almost exclusively originated from a conversation with others. Some are from a good e-book I have read!

My door has always been open for people with start-up ideas and concepts. I take calls, have people come into my office constantly with something new. I believe in being open to everybody at first. Who am I to say what concept is good or bad? Who am I to say what concept is worth pursuing? I can understand people going after an identified market with a new technology. I can however sense when somebody is not improving upon a concept or technology, but just copying someone else. This person is just repeating something or copying verbatim somebody else in the market. Sometimes it makes sense. But often it doesn't, especially if they have no reason why their service will sell or a niche or any defendable position. That concept has to either pivot or fail now. Either way, I keep the people coming. My wife has wondered for years how many people can I go to lunch with, and what is that really all about?

What is Digital Feature Discovery?

Digital Feature Discovery is a process I've been doing whether I intended it or not for a long time. You take a new or existing web or mobile app and "discover" new web and mobile products and services. You find a way to make money with a new or an existing web property. You find a way to turn around an Internet site or app that is not profitable but has some underlying technology worth salvaging. It sounds pretty straight forward. However, it is much more difficult in the real world, because as you will find from reading this book there are a ton of forces of technology, politics and nature working against change in your life, your start-up and organization.

The Digital Feature Discovery process is akin to learning a new language. You need to be fully immersed within all the information available and know your market. You need to know your competitors, your website or mobile app inside and out. You need to get to the point that new services and possibilities emerge whether you are starting up or already in a big company. I have taken past data, trends, an existing website or applications and used this information to create a plan for financial success.

This process can be overwhelming for companies I have worked for and many clients I consult to. The same principles that can be applied to a big IT company, can be applied to start-ups. The only exception here is that the information, methods and processes are not yet existing within the start-up. The data is out there in the external environment. To create a tech start-up you have to take this information and put it together in a workable, profitable manner.

How do you take an old website with an average design, not a lot of sales and tons of traffic and make it hum, sing and most importantly make money? By combining data with trends and just being open minded, you can find new ways to overcome what appears to be a dead end. Often just doing a better job is all it takes. It is not just hard work that counts; it is using creativity, testing and collaboration with a team to figure these things out. And then there are many situations which cannot be changed. I believe it is important to sometimes Fail Fast. If you are going to do it, do it now.

I had a chance when writing this book, to go back to important blog articles I wrote over the years and found important vignettes and points to remember. As far as the quality of the writing. I would only write a book I would like to read myself. To have time to read a book like this to me is a luxury. We are all being overloaded, overstimulated with tons of information in today's smart device world, which makes it difficult to sit back and just read. Everywhere you go, your smartphone, Internet or wearable technology goes with you. At least this means you can bring this book with you.

There are not a lot of original ideas, just a lot of original ways these ideas are implemented and discussed. So don't be surprised if you don't learn anything new if you read this book. You will however, end up remembering old ideas you had in the back of your head, especially if you are a good friend of mine :) It's kind of like patents. Almost all patents are based on parts of other patents, except a patent is a unique combination that creates something new that was not so obvious.

Many times over the last 25 years we have witnessed the technology world change right before our eyes. The first time I realized how serious an impact these changes were having was a day in 1993 when we put the Mosaic browser on my PC at my job at Bell Atlantic Mobile and I was able to surf the web for the first time. Another important event I remember in 1999 was the day AIM, AOL Instant Messenger ended up on my desktop. I downloaded AIM working at an office in North Miami Beach, Florida. I told my brother in New York City to load AIM. Together we had our first text chat. It was a break-through for us, to be able to chat like that without a phone call. Now it is old news. It was really a turning point for most of us that we have forgotten. The basic capabilities to communicate are the most important.

The third time I knew the tech world had seriously changed was when I realized time had been removed as a factor in publishing content online. I had just written a blog article that I was quite proud of in 2009. At the end of writing my blog article, I typically will post it in my WordPress blog and then create a URL for the blog and then post it on Twitter.com @dgudema. Within 1 minute my sister called me to congratulate me on the article I wrote. I felt it was a second! I was wondering how could she have read it so quickly. But then I remember I had connected LinkedIn to my blog, so it popped immediately onto the page as I posted the Twitter entry. She had put the Linkedin app on her phone and she got the push notification. And this is about the time that smart phones had emerged, where users started receiving content literally at lightning speed. And time has been removed as a barrier.

The actual technology is only 20% of what makes a start-up successful.

5 CRITICAL MUST ANSWER QUESTIONS FOR START-UPS

This sections covers the 5 critical questions start-ups must answer. We came up with these questions after interacting with many tech start-ups in the past 2 years at all different levels. This is from an idea with no pitch to the well-funded and at the MPV or Beta Version stage. I use these 5 questions in my tech start-up pitch event I run in Boca Raton, FL for their 3 minute elevator pitch.

Up until recently I have been quite passive when it comes to pushing start-ups this way or that. Who am I to tell you what to do? I don't push because I am also under the belief that I don't know the answer to a lot things (like the mind of a 12 year old person's market). I would say, admitting you don't really know the answer is the first step towards finding an answer to these questions. My proclivity for passivity is starting to wane because quite frankly if you can't answer any of these 5 questions, then you need to go back and start all over again (even if you are in year 2).

I am not a know-it-all, smartest guy in the room. I am just going to question your status quo on what you think will be a successful service, app or product implementation by asking directly the most important questions. You decide if you're answer is acceptable.

An old friend who is involved with a ton of start-ups and I commiserated recently. I said to him, "Remember to be tougher on the next start-up guy/gal, because we often let clients fail because we don't have the inner strength to say, NO, THIS DOES NOT SOUND RIGHT", at the right time and place (which is usually right at the beginning).

We all want to get paid as consultants, developers, lawyers, doctors, but let's do a reality check! To just go along with an idea as a consultant, just to get the business, really sucks. Keeping our mouths shut helps nobody in the end. In fact, the start-up will just fail badly, and quite often we knew why in the back of our heads. We just kept our mouth shut and got the pay check. Even if we are wrong we should question everything about a start-up. It may make it very difficult for some entrepreneurs to hear, but they should start getting used to it early on.

So here are the questions to ask the next start-up you come across, as well as the retorts you need to have in certain cases, so they don't end up on a highway with no exits where the highway just ends:

1. What is your business model or how do you make money?

2. Describe your market size and your customer (personally who they are, what they are like, where they hang out and something tangible about them)?

3. How are you planning on getting to market or getting critical mass?

4. Who are you competing with?

5. Who is in charge? Is there already a problem personality on the management team and who is going to run it and who is standing behind the desk answering the phone all day.

Notice I left out one really important question, what is your product or service? Believe or not, it is way below these 5 questions. Sramana Mitra, a start-up guru, taught me this during a pitch I was giving her. It is important, but not as important as these questions. I am starting to think a product can evolve, pivot, and become something else if it has to. But a great team with the right resources in place can probably overcome any product/service question. A dumb product obviously is a problem, but once again I am not going to be able to tell you what is dumb, successful or not. I was out pitched recently for our start-up social app by a group of kids with a game which blows the head off characters (huh!). They got funded and we didn't. So maybe blowing heads off our mobile app characters' heads is a great product. It sounds stupid, but I don't know. I am not 12!

I originally wrote this article in my blog. I could tell you which answers are right or wrong. But I won't. You need to figure this out yourself. There are definitely wrong answers, like "we are going to bigger and better than Facebook." My answer to that is you are wrong! You need to collaborate and not compete. It was never about competition. You cannot compete with Facebook directly. "Collaborate not compete" is a mantra I picked up from CEO Space. It rings true, especially with Facebook, since you can build an app within Facebook and they are happy to partner with you.

Dan Gudema

There is a difference between following and mimicking. When you follow you improve upon an idea. When you mimic you are just a carbon copy.

START-UP WEB BUSINESS MODELS

In really thinking through a start-up you have to choose a business model. Sounds simple, right? There is a bit of a gotcha that a lot of tech entrepreneurs run into. That gotcha is common knowledge. Sometimes common knowledge is not that common. Because Zuckerberg did it with Facebook. or Gates did it with Microsoft or your buddy down the street did it, doesn't mean you can do it, at least the same way. What worked for one person, may not work for another. Get this in your head before making a business model decision!

Just when it seems like you know something, it does not mean you really understand the economics of why something is working or not working. I ran into many cases around the time of the founding of Facebook and Youtube where copycat entrepreneurs simply created new businesses with the same Facebook features and the same business model! They were just cloning Facebook. Most failed miserably.

Ok, so you are thinking of starting a website. You can be a kid right out of high school, in college or working for a massive conglomerate corporation. It does not matter. You have to be able to understand the business models available in order to choose one!

I talk with a lot of young people about what would be their ultimate idea of a web based business or mobile app they would create as a start-up. I was walking through the mall one day, stopped and chatted with a guy selling phones in one of those kiosks and he and I got to the point where he was telling me, he and his buddies were going to be creating a start-up website. Ah-ha! I listened carefully and provided him my thoughts on their precious gem of an idea. I think we will we hearing these words for many years to come. Why, because there are few barriers to entry!

That's when I started to index and examine the exact business models that exist online. Let's start by looking at these start-up models based on risk vs. reward and the known business models:

1. Advertising – You make money by visitors clicking on links, viewing banners and a few other twists on this original model. No explanation needed. Google Adwords is the way most do it. There are a lot of them out there, a few very successful, but mainly the ones that have gained "critical mass".

2. Product/Service Sales – You sell products and deliver physically or virtually. This can be web or mobile. In the

case of a mobile app, you are selling a piece of downloadable software. No explanation needed. Amazon, Best Buy, Target, Wal-Mart, ACME Catalog Company

3. Membership – You make money (every month) by people joining your site. You know, pay for monthly services to use, view your site.

4. Commission Exchange – You make money whenever a person trades, sells, works, with another person. Ebay, LogoTournament.com, lots of other ones out there.

5. Sponsorship – Basically a twist on advertising, but more than advertising, you get paid no matter the traffic levels, so it is a non-click based advertising.

6. Virtual Business To Business Services – You sell backend services to other business called Saas, Software As A Service. Good examples are Constant Contact, iContact, hosting, chat.

7. Lead Generation - You collect the leads and sell them to a third party. In fact, you control the information flow and set the information price... A good example is Autobytel.

8. Freemium, Coins/Credits – Typical of mobile app games, where you get the app for free, but there are small incremental payments that users need to make along the way to get features or credits.

Risk vs. Reward

I am sure there are about 10 other business models out

there (that are real clever), but this list is pretty much the ones that make sense on the web. And when it comes to risk and reward you have to weigh the chances of your success versus the reward. Remember, not everybody is going to make a billion dollars on their first venture. I say be happy with a million. In fact be happy with quarter of a million. I say just be happy with success, meaning you are a viable business.

So, as you set out to create your new web business, even a new business model, you have to weigh your chances of survival. How to you weigh your chances of survival?

1. Your Track Record

If this is your first time, then reduce the risk by succeeding in ways others have not.

2. Your Capitalization

Often website development is not about revenue, but about staying in business. Having the resources to do it is critical. By resources this is man-power really in the end. Everything else, including hosting is dirt cheap now.

3. Your Talents

If you are not a programmer, your chances of making a successful run at a web business model that is not retail or based on a system to pay for, are remote…unless you are fully capitalized. Being a programmer you have an advantage, saving thousands on programming.

4. Your Ability To Schmooze

Getting others to work for nothing is a talent. Getting partnerships in place to make it happen is a talent. Having an ability to convince others to give you money is even a bigger talent. A god given talent is the ability to sell.

5. Your Tenaciousness

This may be a moot point if you don't have any of the other things above. Keeping at it is important and critical to your success. If you are broke, not a programmer, not a great sales person or networker/presenter and haven't done this before, your tenaciousness may be all you have going for you.

The Personal Analysis

So, you need to look in the mirror and take your idea and go through an analysis. Typically new, unique ideas start with the entrepreneur saying I am going to create this really cool site. For instance a good example would be a local news blog site. And I am going to make money by advertising sales. Well, good luck. In fact I tell entrepreneurs, the quickest way to fail is relying solely on advertising sales. I believe that you will have to generate a million visitors a month to make something like $50,000 a year on the click through dollars. You can do this, but it is a long shot at best.

Remember most click thru's are paying GOOGLE the money, not you. You get a percentage of clicks, and you are not in control of the ad networks, Commission Junction, Google, Yahoo, AOL and others. The big boys in the ad business already take a hefty fee, from the little that is made on ads, and they have a heavy hand in control already. So get it out of your head that the ad model is your model unless you are going for the million to one lottery ticket! Ad models are high risk, but high reward. Many try. Few make it big. Ad models like Facebook and others prove both that you can do it, but the chances are unlikely. Chances of that happening are like 10 million to 1…in my mind. Why take that risk, when you can work on the sure thing.

So, then you say, well my local blog can be a membership site… Sounds good, and in fact if you can find a way to get people to pay, you are going to be in the money. Not a lot of members paying monthly will make a million dollars a year in revenue. If you had 10,000 members paying $9 a month, you have a million dollar revenue site. So this is more of what you need to be thinking about. I give you a 1 in a 500 chance of surviving with a membership model… If you do, you will profit nicely.

Then there is the back-end model. We also call this Software As A Service (Saas). If you get it rolling, you will get monthly or periodic payments, so it is a very similar model to membership. I will give you a 1 in 25 chance of survival in this model, because it is business to business and businesses need help online!

The market exchange with commission model is really dependent on your technical know-how and luck. Choose the right model and you could hit it big like eBay. My odds of success are 1 in 10,000. So not so good, but who knows, it is a big payoff model like advertising, so you are either out of business or a billionaire.

Finally the retail online model is a medium (and potentially high) reward and lower risk. You can make it well enough if you have the talent and luck. If you don't have the talent and are new to online business you still have a chance, but it is risky as well. Knowing your product is everything and if you do know a product well, you may be in luck. I think the prospects of becoming a billionaire in retail are low, but my odds are about 1 in 10 will make some money. Hey, Jeff Bezos and Amazon did it!

Lead Generation

If you pursue this model, there is about a 1 in 30 chance in my mind of making a good living. It is possibly an amazingly good pay off as well. This is especially true if you choose the right industry with the right payout. Every store, sales rep in the world needs leads, so this is a great place to start as well.

Coins/Credits

I have taken a careful look at coins and credit business models. They tend to work better on mobile applications. I personally have never paid for any coin or credit. However, I believe millennials and future generations will adopt it more than I will. Therefore, I highly recommend it, depending on the market. I would give you a 1 in 100 chance of making it though. That's because I see 500,000 app on the iTunes app store. How are you going to differentiate yourself there?

I put this section in the book just to get your creative juices flowing.

10 WEB BUSINESSES I WOULD START IF I WERE IN COLLEGE

If I was in college today, and the University of Maryland was over 25 years ago for me, I would be looking at the world through a prism of the possibilities, not the world of high unemployment.

While the Tea Partiers, Democrats, and everybody in between is often castigating the economy for their lost job (and I want my country back stupidity), I am saying wait a second. I look at the true reality for a tech savvy college kid, and I can come up with at least 10 businesses I would start right now. You could probably come up with 100. It is one of the best times to be a college kid and start a small business and we should promote them to do so. There are hack-a-thons and start-up weekends happening in every major city and on every major college campus in the US. It is not just a movement, it is an entire generational shift towards digital entrepreneurialism.

For a 40-something person, about to turn 50, like myself it all seems gloom and doom. For those in retirement or about to get to retirement, it is even gloomier. We are perhaps about to enter into a 20 year cyclical downturn that may match the Japanese downturn from 1990 to now… This means potentially deflation, a double, triple dip recession, which kind of looks like a group of parabolas you could call a depression when you get right down to it.

So, why would I start these businesses if I were in college?

Because, in the middle of all this doom and gloom, there is a glimmer of hope. We are, as you know, in the most connected period, because of the internet and mobile devices that man has ever been in. We are at the precipice of greatness and capability for those who can capture it. With just a Mac Book or iPad and a wifi connection we have the world at our feet. The glass is truly half full. You just have to reach out and grab it.

Also interestingly enough I get a request to be an intern from a college grad or student every once in a while. I don't have time for them. If you had sent me a proposal to do some business that helps me either increase sales or reduce costs, then we may have a conversation. Be bold, not helpless. Be at my level, not beholden to anyone.

Here are my ideas for college student businesses.

1. Customized Scrapbooks

If I was a young lady in college and had the desire, this is an easy one to get into. Just advertise on your web page that you will put together a physical or virtual scrapbook for people from their online photo albums (would be nice to have a physical book), and you will do a wedding, bar mitzvah, graduation, birthday, etc.

   Skills you need for this service:
   - ability to be able put a listing on Craigslist
   - ability to know how to use Picassa, Flickr, Facebook?
   - know how to work with scissors and glue?
   - have a sense of design…
   - lots of friends and relatives to test out your service.

2. Website Testing Service

This is where you fully test out stated and production websites for companies for a small fee. There is one big competitor out there, can't remember their name. But there is room for more, a lot more companies that test things like usability, browsers working with new functions.

What you need for this service:
   - Probably a good idea to have a website.
   - be detailed oriented.
   - know how to SEO your site, know Craigslist, know some online marketing.
   - a good game player probably would do good here.
   - go to networking parties, meetings locally to find clients.

3. Substitute Game Player/Substitute Person Online

I hear that there are gamers out there, who are hired to be some rich kid's substitute, while they are out and about. If it is not games, you can hire yourself out to be somebody or monitor things for people. Some people may actually want somebody else to go through their mail and monitor the details.

What you need for this business:
- be an excellent gamer.
- ability to use Craigslist and Facebook for promotion.

4. Verification Services

There are tons of verification services out there, and people pay them all the time to verify who somebody sales who they are. But essentially, in the end, nothing is stopping you from going into the business. Look at the dating business these days, everybody needs small time private detective services. And being local, a real local kid who can check up on things is an opportunity to get paid.

What you need for this service:
- learning google, yellow pages, white pages
- ability to read a map, know how to call people
- some social engineering skills (good on the phone)
- ability to use craigslist and Facebook, maybe a website.

5. iPhone/SmartPhone Glass Fix it Now Service

While there is a guy already fixing phones at every corner in America, it is not yet too late to jump in the fray with a new service, especially on campus. I happened to break my iPhone glass and I went to a guy at the mall to fix it for like

$79 bucks…

What you need for this service:
- Contact Apple, look for companies with fix it materials online.
- dexterity
- ability to work with glue
- ability to get flyers around town, maybe a billboard, use the free space.

6. Cellphone Reseller Service

Everybody has these old phones. Your job is to go around and buy the old ones, for very little and resell them to those who want them. Turns out that a used iPhone is worth a pretty penny. Refurb them, do what you have to with wipes…

What you need for this service:
- Ability to work with Mr. Clean wipes
- Ability to put up flyers with ads, and be creative.
- Ability to negotiate.
- Ability to work with ebay.

7. Lead Generation Services

Lead generation means taking somebody's information and selling it to others who want. How do you start? You need to find a client or industry that needs leads. Examples are many, including local restaurants, car dealers, car wash, insurance, online colleges, organizations, cruises, airlines, websites (big one). Just ask what they will pay for a lead, and then go and get the leads.

What you need for this service:

- Good business sense (something I have lacked over the years)
- Good with managing data (Excel, google docs for newbies)
- Good negotiating skills.
- Creativity.

8. Skype After Hours Service

This is an old business, but it can be reborn in the world of Skype. Let's say there is a website and that website only has hours between 8am and 5pm. Let's say you are around from 5pm till midnight. You have the website state that they have after hours, using Skype. They list your skype number, which should also be Video, and if the customer misses something during the day, you take notes from the customer and leave it for the website. This is new twist on a very old phone service. Funny thing is the video skype service is probably better than most ecommerce companies current non-video offering.

What you need for this service:
- PC, notebook with webcam and mic.
- a decent shirt, no nudity.
- ability to use email and skype.
- a clean space to get the call, no ugly dorm room background. not sure how to make this happen, but it needs to be professional enough.

9. Lease It

This business model came to my attention when I ran into a local kid leasing books the local college. Turns out this business is booming, both nationally through big sites and on campuses around the country. So you probably have heard of this one. This leasing deal turns out to be a pretty good solid couple thousand dollar a semester business if run well. And it goes way beyond books, perhaps lease play stations, Wii's, maybe others only want these things for the weekend and don't want to own or store it themselves.

What you need for this concept:
- some storage space.
- negotiating capability.
- ability to put up flyers and create a website.
- contacts and friends

10. Help By The Skype Hour

This is just a shot in the dark, but once again the old 900 number concept maybe on its way back, except this is using Skype. You need however, to not take the call until they have completed the paypal payment. What are you going to sell... Hmm, lots of things to sell help on... On a college campus I would say: Choosing Classes, Math Tutoring, English Tutoring, Game Tutoring (maybe) and any other knowledge you got. If people need it, they will buy it. I would say a brush up tutor service right before finals may be the way to go on this one. And the Skype part is probably a new twist on this.

What you need for this one:
- ability to set up and use skype.
- some kind of skill.
- ability to use craigslist, dorm boards, school paper.
-ability to set up Paypal.

A man runs into a famous rabbi as he walks across an airport. He says "Rabbi Levi by chance". The rabbi stops and answers "There is nothing in this world that happens by chance".

TECH MIND VS. BUSINESS MIND

Being that I am an engineer mind, I tend to start with the product and not the market when thinking of a start-up. This is a big mistake. You have to start with the market in mind. The ability to even change how our minds work has so many implications for programmers and kid entrepreneurs I meet with. They all want to start a small tech internet company and want to succeed but just can't seem to get their tech start-up right.

A lot of this is because tech guys like me want to find something cool and make it themselves, which could even be a worse decision. We like the tech side of things, not the marketing side. And though it is not a hard and fast rule used in making decisions on what business to go in, determining the market potential is still the make or break point of deciding what business to go into. Most of us techies just have a cool idea, but have no clue of the potential value of the concept or project. We don't know who or what is willing to pay for it. Among the successful, there are those who figure this out right away and there are those who just get lucky being in the right place at the right time. The right timers are the ones to watch out for, since they think they know something. The second time around is not always the same!

A Miniscule Market Inside Of An Even Tinier Market

Getting together for lunch with one of the early start-up team members of JDate.com/Spark Networks, we found some common ground discussing the issue of being in a start-up with a small market, and how this just limits what you are doing and that can kill the potential for investors. It is important to choose your market wisely, and often techies don't understand the market. They just want to start coding. For instance, the dating industry is generally speaking not the greatest sized market overall. I am referring to market size by measuring how much revenue a year markets can produce. I believe the dating industry is a $2 billion dollar market a year globally (and though I use the word billion… it is not a good word when it comes to markets, because you never get 100% or even 10%, we are often lucky to get 2% market share). E-commerce sales is over a $4 trillion a year market globally and that market is terrific! And if you were to create a Jewish dating site within the dating business, that will pretty much leave you with a $30 million dollar potential market size and basically 95% of that is already going to JDate, so what is your Total Addressable Market (the possible chances of a market)? It's really crap for creating THE next Jewish dating site since you will not unseat the leader It could be a $5 million market, of which maybe you can capture 5%. That is looking like $250k a year in revenue as your max potential and with an employee and a 40% margin... Get a real job. It will pay more! Really not a place you want to go!

So, Why Do People Jump Into Crappy Markets?

This is where the tech mind overcomes the business mind! I know, I have done it several times. Techies and rational people get caught up in not the revenue size but the finesse of the project. They love how cool would it be to do x, y or z. Or you have no marketing skills at all or you ignore the exit signs on the highway. I guess we like to hear ourselves talk in the mirror about a cool technology. Or you like to tell people what cool problem you solve. Maybe we are just fixing a problem that we face personally! And yes tons of cool problems can be solved with tons of cool technical solutions, but the facts are the facts, market size is market size. I had an MBA finance professor at Farleigh Dickinson in Madison, NJ who looked around the room and asked us what industry we worked in. I was in Telco, and he said "maybe". Some people were school teachers, he shook his head "no". Stock broker, he shook his head "no". As soon as somebody said they worked in the pharmaceutical business he simply said, "I don't care if you are going to be the bottom secretary, stay in that industry and you will retire rich..." Point is, choose your market wisely. Yachts and golfing are terrific markets for instance!

A Product In Search Of A Market

This is where tech guys and gals like me start. We start with a cool thing and try to apply it to markets. Stop right there! Now, sometimes a cool invention or technology accidentally finds a market, but 90% of the time it does not! Me thinks I can take a piece of web code in this market and shove it into that market. I implore you to start over when it comes to your product, not just switch the website around or change the coding framework. I have done this as well. You have to start with the money each time you have a new product and figure out the market size. What are they willing to pay for it? What is it worth to the customer? What is the asset value you are creating? What is it worth? What intangibles are you creating?. There needs to be some consideration of the asset you will be creating and what that will be worth to a buyer. But we are not talking about customers now, we are talking about competitors and buyers of software companies! Creating a tool that needs to be acquired by a Google or another company is another form of measuring the market before creating the technology. In fact asset selling, not revenue is the number one way techies make it big.

The Socratic Within ME

Now I am going to reverse directions a bit and give you the upside of being a techie and starting with the technology. Using tech sometimes you can figure out a path to the market. I wrote a blog article on "Why I Don't Really Know Anything". It's in the chapter How to Respond to New Ideas. It proves that there could be something within the techie cool thing you have been building that can be re-purposed for something real and marketable. But you have to start from scratch in terms of the final product. You simply have to match a problem you are solving with different markets, and keep applying the problem to different markets until you find a market size that is profitable.

Now you may have to stay in a niche. I recently met the founder of Veggidate.com (yes for vegetarians) and its small, but it is as good a niche to as any. So, let's start again with the dating site. So you still have not given up on the Jewish dating market. You are determined. You are a programmer and you don't listen well. The only way of succeeding I can think of is you need to introduce your product in a new and growing market with a new technology. Mobile is a good example. Find a new market entry point like events. Find a new methodology like through education. Re-enter the market through a new medium. That may work. Because you were able to conquer one of these three markets that JDate site does not have ownership of, you would be able to get maybe a smidgen of a market. More importantly, your company would be on the target list of successful businesses they are looking to buy along with a bunch of other people obsessed with serving a small market just because you like to… But leave your expectation for financial success at the door.

President Lincoln lost eight elections, twice failed in business and suffered a nervous breakdown before becoming President of the United States.

LEARNING TO FAIL FAST THE HARD WAY

What Is Failing Fast?

Simply put, failing fast means you find out right away that your idea, concept, new product is a dud, so you can either stop what you are doing or make some serious corrections. But failing really means failing, and it generally means giving up earlier in the process. It's a good thing, and something like 90% of tech companies I run into ignore. Tech guys hold fast to their concept way beyond when it was time to give up. I know, I am one of these guys.

Start-ups Need To Fail Faster

I have read a lot of start-up books on the market out there. Most have the same exact answer. You need to fail as fast as possible with new tech concepts. Trust me, this is a definite area I have completely failed at personally, and I have even followed around other people's failing ideas like a pig stuck in the mud. A lot of this is because of a lack of experience. All that corporate experience I gained over the years do not count, because what you need for a start-up is not what you need for a corporate gig. Smarts for a tech start-up is not the same as in other endeavors. The real way to succeed is to be a business person, not a tech person first.

Failing Even Bigger And Slower

But I think failing fast is not just a concept for start-ups. In most big companies they have made failing slow an art form. To be 80% more efficient corporations should stop wasting their time with concepts that could have failed earlier. If they did this, billions would be saved. In fact, entire industries have disappeared because corporations were pursuing failing concept for years. It keeps lots of us employed, but it is oh so annoying. I was talking with somebody about a large tech company acquiring a small tech company recently. What typically happens next is typically complete paralysis. It's like a big corporate giant eats the small company and then anything that resembles change become nearly impossible or so institutional that nobody wants to fail at anything. So how can you fail fast in that situation.

Smaller Means Nimbler

So this is where small start-ups have an advantage. Before blowing millions or billions, a small tech start-up can take a few small actions to end the hypocrisy and stupidity early on. They can create a prototype or barely working product and find out from customers if they are going to pay, use it or whatever they need to prove the market works. Even that may have the unintended consequence of telling the entrepreneur to go ahead with a product or service, when they should have just failed right there. Let's say you interviewed the wrong people who told you the wrong information. Well, you still have a chance to fail early, just not as early.

Misread Market Size

Now that I know better, it is best to start with market size, not product or even customer to determine if you should stop now and fail fast. Let's say you have created a great service that a few people love, and while you are not making any money, you know you are doing good for the world and helping people. I will give you an imaginary service, like a mobile app which gives men advice on what to do for the women in their lives and when to do it, like "buying flowers on a Friday gets a 60% approval rating from women vs. Thursday". Ok, cool app, mobile app, even runs and works and all that jazz. But then will people pay for it and how many. So you add it up. Wow, if I collect 50 cents from the 1,000,000 potential real customers, and only .0001 pay, then I will have made $5000 on this venture in total. Well, just fail now! It may have been cool, but trust me I have been involved with a not so profitable business for many years with no exit strategy and it sucks.

Quit, But Don't Always Quit

I am not saying that you should quit your venture right now. I am just saying stop taking years to figure out that there is no money to be made and that you are wasting your time. You should just try to figure this out early on. You need to know what the total market opportunity is. In high-tech I now say when they use the words "Billions" I don't like it. I want to hear the words "Hundreds of Billions" or "Trillions" as far as market size. Sometimes there are many reasons to stay in a business and see it through, but if you see a problem with your concept or your idea and the market does not make sense, then stop now and move on to something which can make you money and make a living.

Thinking Like A Start-Up

Dan Gudema

Web Marketing

In choosing an app name or domain name for your tech start-up there is only one thing that matters, **memorability**.

WEB BRANDING

About 10 years ago I picked up a copy of *Don't Make Me Think* by Steve Krug. It is by far the simplest bible-like book of user interface design. The principle of this short read is simply creating web page layouts that meet common ways people are used to using the web, and you will make your site more usable and successful. And according to Krug, deviations from these norms make people think. Making people think, means they sometimes get confused, sometimes they leave the site and often they don't make the decisions you want them to make. Basically you make people think and that is a bad thing.

Don't Make Me Think Example

A good example in the book is the word "Search" vs.

"Quick Search" on a search form on a website. The slight difference of the wording "Quick Search" actually makes people think for a second, like is this search really quicker, where is the real search? According to Krug, if you are making people think, the sites usability is lessened and therefor things like conversion rates drop and quality of the site is lower. Ok, go and read that book now!

World Famous & Now We Are Starting To Think

I was sitting in on a brand building call by David Tyreman, founder of World Famous Company, a guru extraordinaire on brand building. He was covering the concept of making sure customers are in their comfort zone, whether as they arrive on your site, your business, in between, or right before buying or during the transaction. You can add comfort to all customer experiences! This is part of the larger concept of improving and creating your world famous brand. Go and buy David Tyreman's book as well. It is worth it.

Brand Comfort Zone

This comfort zone covers both physical and virtual spaces. By physical, a good example for our speed dating business is when people are getting ready for a speed dating event. Are they comfortable? Are they happy, at ease, and in the proper zone right before an event? Trust me people are nervously standing around before speed dating, especially looking at people walking in the door, wondering if they are going to be in the event. For a virtual website, have you created an environment on the website that eases the visitors comfort level and therefor improved their comfort zone? An interesting example is Apple.com. They follow a few standards. Often on the Apple.com website, I have to search around and find what to click on and discover stuff. But that is what Apple is all about. It is a tug of war between being Apple (branding) and Making People Not think. Well, this is what I am noticing is a diversion from Don't Make Me Think. In fact, it's the time you want people to think, because you are using your brand to improve their comfort zone.

VictoriasSecret.com's Pink Bag

Back in 2001 or so, I was working at abcdistributing.com, specifically on their website analytics and their cart. abcdistributing.com, which I occasionally talk about in my blog, was the unsung hero of catalog companies that only women who love catalogs knew about. They used to get thousands of orders a day online, so small improvements in their site design made a big difference. I was looking around back then and noticed that Victoria's Secret was the first website to really introduce a different kind of a cart. Theirs was "Add To Bag". Carts were just simply "Add to Cart" or "Buy Now" buttons back then, so when I saw this nicely branded little bag, I was sincerely impressed. It was really my first introduction to how online branding can be extended to comfort zones online. I just did not know it back then. I tried to think of a way to extend this to abc distributing, a business that did not believe in branding, and all I was able to think of was this box they shipped out had this little fish icon on it. Everybody remembered them that way. That was their brand at the time, and therefore I pushed to switch their "Add To Cart" to "Add To Box" with a little box icon... Of course they did not go for it!. Finally, thank you David Tyreman, for explaining to us what this is about!

Be Uniquely The Same

So, in the end what I think this means is not everything online fits into a cookie cutter way of doing things. *Don't Make Me Think* obviously is a great example to start with in building user interface designs. It says don't put something in a place on a site like a search box on the bottom left, or a menu bar in the middle of a page (not at the top), or the company logo in the middle of the page or change wording like About to "Who we are". But there are exceptions, many exceptions, but exceptions that have to do with branding, where you want people to think! Another good example is a client who switched the word "Services" to the word "Benefits". Or a site that uses "Start Your Journey" vs. "Buy Now". So, it appears, good branding, especially improving the customer comfort zone, trumps *Don't Make Me Think*. Sorry Steve Krug, sometimes you gotta think!

Dan Gudema

The number one thing we tell start-ups is find a way to start having revenue. Investors are more impressed with this than any plan you could ever show them.

HOW TO WRITE A STRATEGIC MARKETING PLAN

I was working with a client recently who had brought me in to discuss several aspects of their online marketing program. The big issue I asked the team was what are you currently doing and what is your plan of attack? This company had not actually formally created a plan, and more specifically a strategic or a tactical plan, for online. I found it interesting when they admitted that they did not have a plan they could show me. So, over the next couple of weeks I put one together for them. They are not a typical online company, but they are typical of an offline company; a company that has not yet hit the ground running and developed a specific and prioritized online marketing plan.

My Credentials

Actually, other than my recent MBA and 15 years of web

development and online marketing experience, I have no executive credentials in the online marketing area. What I do have is battle scars of carrying out online marketing objectives for marketing executives. I will say I don't have that much respect for marketing executives. Not sure if that is because they were not the right people for the jobs, or the typical marketing executive in the online world in the last 13 years was an offline marketer, who had moved online and was still not ready for the task at hand. I guess if I had worked for a 20 something exec conquering the world, I may have a different story to tell. Either way, I did work on a site that got 30 million visits a month and 25,000 orders a day and was involved with all aspects of online marketing for that firm for 6 years and I have worked for companies like abc distributing, Victoriassecret.com and Verio/NTT corp. So I have seen a few things here and there. But what probably makes me experienced enough is the fact that I have been involved with start-ups over the past 10 years like Pre-Dating.com and my recent Take It National, and I run into online marketing initiatives head on all the time.

Strategic vs. Tactical Plan

I did a little bit of research and found out that I was going to be writing a tactical plan not a strategic plan. I had mixed these up, but either way, I was going to give them an idea of what to do online and their priorities. Does not matter what you call it. The online strategic plan, none the less, is a higher level plan that determines what you are actually going to sell and to whom. The online tactical plan is the actual detailed areas that the online marketing will cover in order to capture and convert online visitors. Doesn't matter in the end, because what is needed is the tactical plan to do be able to make a decision on what to do.

Not All Plans Are Alike

One thing I realized is this particular business, which I am not going to mention by name, needed a special plan for their needs and not a cookie cutter approach. I think this is one of the mistakes many companies make. By cookie cutter, the marketing department tries to cover every part of their plan equally and applies every recommended standard industry method. Problem is there are now many, many potential online marketing initiatives that I can think of. Some are standard parts of marketing, some are new and some are just a form of technology you can exploit. I am going to list as many as I can here, but the point is, that some of these methods are better for certain businesses than others. So you can't say for certainty that email marketing, for instance, is going to be the most important activity for all businesses (but it is darn close to the top or almost always at the top). A marketing book may tell you that, but you have look at each business holistically, where you break down all the facts and ways to market online and then come up with a plan that makes sense, for THAT PARTICULAR business. If you try to do everything at once, and therefor nothing in a superior way, you may end up with a mediocre outcome and even a misguided outcome, mainly because you want to dot all the I's and cross all the T's of marketing and not really do things strategic justice. Just showing up to work in marketing is not enough these days to do online well. And just reading a list of what to do on this website is still not enough to make the right decisions. In fact you have to start thinking strategically to make a difference today.

All The Online Marketing Methods I Can Think Of

I have broken down all the online marketing methods I can think of, and explain them. Some are what I refer to as vertical methods and some are horizontal, meaning they are methods that span across all the other methods...

1. Create A Website
2. Email Marketing
3. Search Engine Optimization
4. Pay Per Click
5. Adwords
6. Banner Ads
7. Video Marketing (Youtube)
8. Social Media Marketing (Facebook, Twitter, Instagram)
9. Linkedin Marketing
10. Photo Marketing
11. Webinars
12. Chat Sessions
13. Teleseminars
14. Landing Page Marketing
15. Affinity Marketing
16. Affiliate Marketing
17. Lead Generation Marketing
18. Viral Marketing
19. Guerilla Marketing

Well, that's it for now. In the second part of this discussion I am going to explain each of these areas of the plan and why your business should think about focusing on a specific one. I am also planning on discussing how to prioritize and make the right strategic decisions and finally how to not get burned by costly marketing agencies!

Online Marketing Foundation

When I say online marketing foundation, this goes even deeper than marketing, it typically revolves around technology. A lot of marketing executives will go for the jugular in their job and try to achieve, but achievement may not be possible if the basic infrastructure is not in place, Even worse, a serious campaign can be completely a waste if a simple thing like collecting email addresses is not built correctly in the database. One simple case in point, is one company I worked for collected customer names without separating the first and last names in the DB. This was a marketing foundation structural problem. We could not send out the emails in a personalized fashion, because we were not getting the information in the database correctly. Often executives want to tackle the marketing issue head on with a nuclear weapon that has no army structure behind it. If you invade a country and have no plans or ability to manage the situation, you will have chaos. So, this is what is recommended first:

1. Get a great website.

Believe it or not, there are a tiny percentage of companies who market without a great, less a good website. This has to be ready for any campaign. What I mean by great website is one that can spell out your value proposition and contains the customer motivation [for arriving at the site].

2. Get a good, structured email collection method in place.

You need to be able to collect email addresses and

segmenting them would be a good start.

3. Get the ability to allow customers to opt-out.

This is critical before sending your first email campaign. Without it, you may end up pissing off not just people. If you piss off the email providers such as Gmail, Yahoo, Microsoft or AOL, you will have bigger problems.

4. Landing Pages

If you are going to be running marketing campaigns, then specialized landing pages help even more in building out your foundation.

5. Checkout

Now most companies allow customers to buy products online, but if you don't have it in place and you are pushing customers to your site, you need to give them a place to buy.

6. Contact us

We mentioned email collection above, but customers "Don't Need To Think", so they need to be able to easily contact your company.

I am sure there are a lot more structural pieces, but these are a good start. Notice these are part of the online marketing plan, but they are more than that, they are the building blocks for success. You need to make sure these are ready for the high volume of traffic you are going to receive.

Online Marketing Plan Areas Explained

I am going to explain each of these areas of online marketing. Some may not have occurred to be online marketing places for your business, but you may find that they have a greater impact than you would have ever expected. This is where, in my final article, I will get into priorities, and why making certain decisions to go after low hanging fruit, is critical.

Create A Website

No need to say more. You and I know what a website is. Maybe a few people out there think they have a website, because they have a Facebook page. It is close, but not exactly.

Email Marketing

Once again, make sure it is very easy to understand. You get together a message and send it via email to potential or existing customers.

Search Engine Optimization

While many have made this a business, it is simple enough. You make sure your site content, titles, urls and Meta tags are optimized for the search engines, mainly Google today.

Pay Per Click

Once again, everybody pretty much knows this. You pay for each click on a Google or others and it is a bid process based on the highest bidder paying for the click. Google focuses on the top 3.

Adwords

A variation on pay per click, with the variation focused on words showing up on third party content sites, not on the search engines. This seems to be a big one through Google and it is a way to get traffic.

Banner Ads

This is an old standby. It is basically an image that people pay for customers to view and get clicks through. I believe the days of banner ads are coming back.

Video Marketing (Youtube)

A lot of companies don't understand the power of video marketing. Thanks to the relationship between Youtube and Google, which are the same company, video can now be seen much higher in the search engines. The ability to push up video, convert it to flash, comment, tag and search engine optimize your video, this is a high growth marketing area your business may need to take advantage of. I believe it's the future of marketing.

Facebook Marketing

This is really a hot topic right now, as companies are trying to figure out a way to market through social networks. Best part of this type of marketing is the ability to analyze and understand exact keywords and affinity relationships (close relationships) that exist between your product/service and related search terms. Also Facebook marketing harkens back to banner ads and is a rebirth of the banner ad.

Linkedin Marketing

This is just starting and like Facebook will be on a growth area for a while. If your business is B2B then this is where you should be looking to spend your marketing dollars. If you are related to the human resources area, it is pay dirt time.

Photo Marketing

Just like video on Youtube a lot of companies misunderstand the power of photo marketing. You can easily push up hundreds of photos to Picassa (once again a google property :) and then name, tag, categorize, geotag and comment on these photos. This information will get indexed on the search engine. This is a low hanging fruit of online marketing and a place, if you have access to images, you need to be!

Webinars

Killer webinars are coming to your town and if you don't act now you will lose out. Apparently make products and services need to be shown through a demo. But there is something out there today that will prepare your webinar in advance so that it does not have to be live. It can be almost on demand. Ever notice that during a TV ad they are giving out a url to watch their webinar (especially pharmaceuticals). This is a great advertising medium for specialized products and services, like health related and that is where your business should be spending its dollars.

Chat Sessions

We were investigating chat sessions way back in 2001 when they came to market. Some online businesses I know live off the marketing capability of chat sessions and convert most of their traffic via chat sessions. Don't under estimate the power of this technology and it is getting more sophisticated as time goes by. The day is coming when Skype enters this market and you will be able to video chat with any customer!

Teleseminars

Just like video seminars, teleseminars are easy to put together, and unlike webinars, teleseminars can easily be accessed. So there for the conversion rate of teleseminars will be much higher, because people can listen easily at work, on the road or anywhere they feel like it. Ignore this area and you will miss out on a lot of low hanging fruit.

Landing Page Marketing

This is just a reminder that any website can go out and create a landing page separate from the site home page. Now, place that landing page on a separate domain name, with an optimized title and now you have a new way to gather traffic. Initially landing pages were for emails, but they are not that way anymore. They can be for search engines, seminars, events, webinars, teleseminars, even SMS. You keep it this way for many reasons, some of which is a specialized campaign for that medium. Either way, you control the medium and using landing pages is a great way to do it. Use a product out there like

HiConversion.com and you are set!

Affinity Marketing

Affinity Marketing is not a vertical technology, but rather a horizontal method of approaching online marketing. It refers to finding relationships with your current customer base. I like to use the free and cheap Quantcast.com to figure these relationships out, but you could go to Nielsen's/Jupiter or Hitwise or others and buy the expensive demographic data. Either way, if you search at Quantcast.com you will find that people who visit your site or your competitors also visit sites X, Y and Z, and that's how you figure out there is an "Affinity" between your site and there's. This is important in deciding where and how to advertise in the long tail [for longer pay per click phrases].

Affiliate Marketing

Affiliate marketing, which I now akin to AdWords, was the old place we used to give out URLs with codes and pay out to sites and people who drive traffic. I personally don't find it to be a very effective way to market for certain products. For dating products, like my old speed dating business, affiliate marketing was not just important, it was the life blood. So, this really depends on the type of business you are in! If it is more personal than commercial, sometimes it makes sense. Commission Junction is still one of the big players, but I am seeing this area slowly disappearing from the big sites out there.

Lead Generation Marketing

When the old ad "Win A Free iPod" came out a couple years ago, lead generation marketing had hit an apex. It is still quite a big field unto itself. You can buy leads from other people who will sell them to you, especially in businesses like Cruise Lines, Online Education, Mortgages and Online Car Buying. I mention these four, because all four are the hottest lead gen markets known on the web just about. Meanwhile, your lead generation yourself needs to be taken care of first!

Viral Marketing

This is an old area of marketing. Remember the ad, "And She Had Two Friends, And She Had Two Friends, And She Had Two Friends". Viral marketing really can work if you enable people to do it. We used to have the old "Tell A Friend" page. That's old hat. Now you have these Gmail, Yahoo, AOL, Linkedin, Facebook login apps, which allow you tell your whole world about whatever you are doing. Viral marketing is the basis of social media marketing!

Guerilla Marketing

Guerilla Marketing takes us in a whole new direction. It was really popular a few years ago, when the old had to be seen video got passed around or the famous cartoonists about George Bush came out. I see Guerilla marketing as a crazy, underground way of getting your product or service out and it is still possible online to do it. Things can grow like wildfire if they are funny or somehow are a "Got To Be Read or Seen Situation". Seems like the only stuff I get like this these days are Tea Party crazy friends of mine sending me stupid diatribes about the world ending!

Mobile/Smart Device Marketing

This area of marketing is just getting started. I am seeing newer and newer technologies showing up on my Ipad, and all are banner ad or video based. Sorry Google, text links are old technology on the Ipad, and it seems like people want the image or video ads. Just having an app to download is part of this marketing effort, and if you supposed to be in the cutting edge you should have an Ipad, Android and Windows Smart Device compatible app.

Blog Marketing

Even though I do blog a lot using WordPress, I think this area may be a little overblown. Do this area right and you will get a lot of visits, especially if you master tagging, categorization, titles, metas and get posted out to all the right RPC servers in the blogosphere… If your product/service requires a little more explaining or some leadership in your industry, this is a key area of your business. Remember though, it is not a foundation. You need to have a site and checkout and email collection to do this right!

Twitter Marketing

If you have ever used TinyUrl.com, you know all about twitter marketing. We hear a lot about marketing through Twitter, but Twitter in some ways is really another form of viral marketing, where you can push out a product release or some other message to your customers or potential customers in a PUSH fashion. I say push, because things like blogging and tweeting are all about push. You push, instead of pull, which is the old search engine methodology. Therefor it is a bigger bang for your buck. But remember once again, no foundation, no orders, make no money…

The more I think about writing a plan for a company's online marketing efforts, I think about all the cookie-cutter, repetitive actions taken out there by thousands and thousands of website owners and marketers. This means people are starting to following standards in online marketing and trust me there are many things you should do and are doing right now! But, in a few cases, I've noticed that some things in marketing are much more important and easy to do than others, and just because everybody else is doing it, doesn't mean you have to do it or should be putting resources into it. Just because the other kids are doing it is not enough…

What I am talking about is making strategic decisions about what is not just easy, but what is going to give you the biggest bang for your buck. Now, that is a very important part of the online marketing plan, such as what to first and then next, and so on. But even before many things can be done, there is and always will be a lot of extra setup work. If you want to have an email marketing campaign system in place, you need to at least have a solution to collect emails, possibly segment them, store them in a database, and then find an email sending solution, and then analyze and follow up. But you can't get ahead of yourself, in that the pillars of a successful part of your marketing may revolve around the SEQUENCE in setting things up. If you just started sending out marketing email, because you were not patient, from the same server as your business correspondence communications (things like receipts, support and customer interaction) and have not come up with a separate domain for sending your email, you may have gotten things out of sequence… Not the end of the world if you are a start-up, but if you had separate domains you were sending from, you would have protected your business correspondence (your real world important email) from getting black-listed.

So for each area of marketing you need to accomplish for your website, I use a rating system for the priority, ease of implementation, time to implement, and other factors. Then based on these additional factors the priority may change. For instance, getting online with a website is still at the top of this list. One thing that is just as easy is creating videos which are nicely tagged and have content on Youtube pointing back to your site. The same thing with easy to implement blog software like WordPress or Blogger, which also points back to your site for SEO (Search Engine Optimization) purposes. So things have changed in online marketing over the years. What was first things first 10 or 5 years ago is not the same. Video and Blogs are now ground zero…not necessarily email… Email is important and the core, but it is a layer now above the website, videos, blogs, picture and other stuff you can easily use to draw traffic. What you have to infer from this, is it is a hell of a lot easier to get out a video camera and make a Youtube video than getting a great email campaign in place. Email campaigns mean more HTML, images possibly, landing pages, etc.

So as part of your prioritization in your online marketing plan, you need to come up with all the ways you are going to market online and focus in on a few quick wins. This is especially true if you want to make something happen now.

Everything these days is about now, not later. Yes, some marketing efforts will take some time, but things like fixing a domain name to all be www. or buying a domain name can be done today. Things like fixing a title per page or a url per page can be done now, not later.

Help Is On The Way

Like I have said in my previous parts of writing a strategic online marketing plan, there are many, I mean many SEO and marketing firms out there to deliver your marketing program. But, there few, like me, who actually act as your marketing exec and help you write a plan. It is the writing of this plan you can't leave to a one trick pony SEO firm. It needs to be an in-house, maybe a consultant like myself, developed thing that represents you and your business. Contact me at @dgudema if you want more info.

Just Say No

You can just say no to cookie-cutter marketing approaches, because quite frankly what is good for the gander may not be good for the goose. If you are a law firm, then how you do marketing is different than an online store. Don't fall into a trap that they are all the same, everybody needs to do the same thing. The only reason you may hear this programmed thinking from your marketing expert/SEO guy/gal is, that is what they know. What "THEY KNOW" is a common problem in the online world, because we are all limited to what we know? One time I went around and asked a dozen different programmers what language to use. Each one gave me a different language because that is what they know. They each told me "the truth" that the language they knew was the one and only to use and the best! What a programmer "only" knows is not a guide to what you need to do and in what sequence you need to do it. For marketers the same is true. We are only as good as what we know, and we can't know everything, less a majority of things! Plus, making these critical "thinking decisions" is a task for a VP of online marketing, not a third party SEO firm. Remember if you own the website, you use marketing firms to carry out your plan, and rarely do they have what it takes to "tell you" the plan and tell you what to do. If you are still at a loss higher a strategist like myself and get a plan! Control over your marketing and what you are doing is important and starts from home base (internally) not externally.

Herding The Cattle

There are many ways to cut a cake and marketing is that cake. I recently ran into a technique being used for website marketing to seniors and they had removed all website links, forcing the seniors to go down ONE and ONE SINGLE path. There was only one way to go through their homepage and it required entering an email address… Why this restriction? What was going on? Well, after I noticed they were using Google Optimizer, an A/B and Multivariate testing tool, I realized they must know something and they tested and in fact it may be a smart move for them. Did the senior really want to go in many directions/places and the answer was maybe not. Maybe 5% were pissed off and left, but the numbers may be high in the conversion rates on those who entered their email address and stayed. This was about herding the cattle, and it raised some interesting psychological issues with website marketing. Some things may be counter intuitive and not straight forward. How do you figure this out? You have to test!

Testing

In the prioritization should be some testing. You don't know everything. So you test. Testing is cheap and easy on the web today. Use Survey Monkey's free service or $50 in a pay per click account. Put up a page to find out if people click through or fill in a form. This is the best way to go about figuring out what works.

Never sell with your own wallet.

INSECURE FOCUSED VS. SECURE UNFOCUSED

Back in 2001 I met my future speed dating site partner at the Association for Internet Professionals in Fort Lauderdale, Florida. A few months later he asked if I could develop in PHP a speed dating website for him that could run events in multiple cities, run by multiple event hosts. By mid-2002 we were in 15 cities and growing fast. Pre-Dating.com went on to be the largest speed dating business in the US, in over 100 US and Canadian markets and was sold in 2004 to Cupid.com.

One issue that I observed working with this partner is he would often overload the home page with tons of details and he went on to write an enormous FAQs page. He was concerned about the customer not having enough information to make a decision to sign up. He had questions in there like "What should I Wear To The Event?", "Where Should I Go Afterwards", "What Happens If It Snows?" And we also had several clicks till a person could actually purchase the speed dating event.

I told my partner that my preference would be to have the registration form right on the home page and to not have all this cluttered text and information and links on that home page, so that it would be clear to me how to buy.

So a few years later I realized that he and I had two differing ways of surfing a website and that is why we had a different opinion of the checkout process. In 2009 I was certified by Marketing Experiments with a Landing Page Optimization Certification and went through their quite amazing training on optimizing web forms and step by step usability methods. So, I do have a background in this area now. Back in 2001 I was simply the web developer.

We can actually take our two ways of thinking and segment the market of surfers into Insecure Focused and Secure Unfocused. If you are going to segment and don't know what they are when you first build your app or site, this is one way of segmenting and serving these two unique audiences. Years ago at another large ecommerce company we segmented on new vs. existing, which is another common way to go. But the Insecure Focused, Secure Unfocused is a psychographic we discovered, making it a good way to segment.

Insecure Focused

Insecure Focused are people that surf a website and have a

lot of concerns about buying and need to have these issues overcome by selling the customer and providing enough information to get them to be "secure" about their feelings of buying. These are people who are concerned about the site being a rip off and not providing or living up to the standard that they are reading about. These people sometimes go as far as reading the terms on a website and they will read all the fine print. I am not sure of the % who fit this segment are who visit your website, because each site will be different. Let's just say that the Insecure Focused person most likely has to leave the website and think about buying before checking out the competition sites, the better business bureau and mulling over it in their bed overnight…

Secure Unfocused

Secure Unfocused people are just that. They are confident in taking a risk on a website, and generally have arrived at that website for a purpose that they knew in advance they would jump at. Basically think of these people as having tunnel vision. Their eyes lock on to an actionable part of the website page and if it makes sense they take action. People like me don't read everything and if we do, we often miss some of the details. It is like the whole page on the site other than the actionable items gets fuzzy. Some people have laughed at me when I say to put an email box saying "get on our list" on their website, even if there is no reason to get on the list. These secure unfocused folks will jump on the list. Some will do it with no call to action at all! It was just there. I had been working on Websites.com for Verio/NTT Corp and put a box on it like this and several months later we had a couple thousand emails.

I am a secure unfocused person. I will basically not want to take the time to read everything. I am a sign up kind of guy. I don't believe it's worth my time to read all those terms and if the deal looks decent enough, I just jump in and get it. Thus, we end up with sites for Secure Unfocused people like Woot.com. Woot.com is one of my favorites.

So, as a web manager you have to say to yourself, where do my beliefs lie? If you are Insecure Focused, then you have to not just design a site you would use, you have to solve the problem for quickies like me who don't want to read everything. If you are a Secure Unfocused type of person, you have to understand that there are people who look at a big form box with fear and trepidation and will never put their email in… unless you coax them. You need to create a path for success for both types of visitors.

There are two mantras for site visitors to consider here, Insecure Focused and Secure Unfocused, in addition to a many other ways to segment. But overall this way is a very actionable way to design for both types of individuals and solve both paths towards successful conversion.

Dan Gudema

Conventional wisdom is very uncommon.
                    Franc Nemanic

OUR DECREASING NEED TO REMEMBER ANYTHING

Years ago in the not so distant past there used to be these little black books we all carried around that held in them names, addresses and phone numbers. Ah, yes we called them address books and phone books. To those of us not well endowed with the gift of memorization, these little books were very, very important. Ok, you know I am being facetious. I am taking about an Address Book. Along with the demise of these little black books (I personally see the iPhone/iPad as the death knell), there is also a big trend, in fact a marketing trend, that we don't need to remember much about who we know anymore, like addresses and numbers. Why is this important? Well if you look at the recent trend of social bookmarking, social media and sharing sites, like Addthis.com, you are seeing a new paradigm emerging where we don't need to know this contact information anymore. In other words, social networking and other kinds of sites are now the conduits for our contact information. The question is how and why you can capitalize on this trend.

Phone Numbers, Cell Phones & PDAs Start The Know Nothing Trend

Let's step back a bit. I had been in the cell phone business back in the 90s, when the first internal phone books emerged. They were good and you could choose from a list of people to call, but when you lost your phone or upgraded, you had to go through the pain of moving your contacts to the new phone. But long before cell phones and landline phones the old phone companies had those 10 digit numbers you had to remember. I am saying "had" because I believe phone numbers one day will be so obfuscated; you won't need to know a number. In fact maybe you just say a name and your smart device finds that person.

It's All In The Palm

When the Palm emerged (how soon we forget) it had all kinds of contact information apps on it. When the Palm merged with a cellphone, we were ecstatic. We would no longer need to keep that little black book for phone numbers. We still had to keep the address book around for the written addresses and some emails at that time. In the late 2000s as the cell phones got smarter, we were able to keep our contact list on our cell phone and integrate lists eventually with things like Google and Gmail. This made it possible when I lost a cell phone to get back at least an old copy of my contacts. But we were not free of having to remember some information.

Tell-A-Friend

As a little side note here, we had put the Tell-A-Friend page on almost every site we built up until 2007. The problem of course with Tell-A-Friend is, if you don't remember their email address, then you couldn't tell a friend. So how close a friend were they? So in the early years of the web, you remembered all your friend's email addresses and if you didn't, you copied and pasted it from your email program. But this is where the little black book came out.

Google Throws A Life Line

Gmail was the first really great implementation of a technology that naturally offered up contact information, such as email addresses and names of previous email contacts in a way that was unobtrusive. It used a natural intelligence that was not dorky or difficult and did not bother you. Using my Gmail account, I would just start to type either an email address or a name and it would show the contacts I needed. You could still search Gmail and find it other ways. Now, the geeky at-heart will email me and tell me that there were others before Gmail with this capability. I am sure of that. But this is the place I remember losing my "email" mind and not having to add online email addresses to my little black book. I think it was around 2003 or so for me, but it doesn't matter. What is important is I don't know your email address if you asked me now!

Make It So Linkedin! Now We Don't Have To Remember Ourselves

The emergence of Linkedin.com is much more than just a place for our business info and contact info. It created a place where we could put our resume information and not really have to maintain a physical resume. We are not totally there yet, but it is the beginning of another little piece of paper shoved into my little black book going away. The critical aspect of LinkedIn is it allowed people to change jobs, lose their primary email address, and keep in contact with you regardless.

If you are "Linked-In" with somebody, they can change their email address and life is good again. You don't lose them. Next time you login to LinkedIn they have a different email address but life goes on just the same for your contact relationship. And the ability to use LinkedIn to communicate to you with "send them a message" changed the game. This small innovation in the business world has made it so even my little Gmail artificial intelligence is not that important anymore. The ability to contact and communicate within these types of applications was well underway with the big daddy of them all coming to town, Facebook.com

Social Networks, Honey Where'd My Brain Go?

So now that Facebook is upon us and seemingly consuming 90% of the online time of people who seem to have all the time in the world for Facebook, a second phase of this trend is now kicking in. We no longer need to remember not just phone numbers or email addresses. We don't even have to remember our friend's names. When you share a link or webpage on the web and you use one of the many sharing mechanisms, like Facebook, Gmail, Twitter, Vimeo, and there are others, life has gotten easy to ping somebody. If you use Facebook sharing to share you can send your message by searching by a physical face Icon now! That conceptually means that you don't need to remember anybody's name anymore. And I see this trend increasing as Facebook logins, what we call Oauth, an ability to login with Facebook, Twitter and Linkedin, and other types of sharing mechanisms seem to be everywhere these days. Let's face it. All you have to do is click a social network button to create an account on most sites now. For the insecure unfocused among us, this is heaven!

The Final Frontier: Smarter Devices Means You Can Be Even Dumber!

When you got your first iPhone and you logged in to iTunes, and you downloaded your first Angry Birds app, the trend became apparent. You did not have to enter your email address each time. Just enter a password. Apple knows who you are; your contact info and basically we don't need to know ourselves (email-wise). The whole concept of remembering your email address is becoming less important. Once you are on an iPad you don't need to enter your email address to get on a list with an app. You buy things through iTunes. And if you use Words With Friends by Zynga you interact with people that you don't really know and your contact info is embedded somewhere on a hard drive in the cloud ("the keyword for basic hosted hard drive storage now!"). Smart devices are making it so we don't need to even know who we are. We could just all become zombies in the apocalypse and our wearable computers will know who we are!

What's Next?

Well, I have no crystal ball, but obviously Facebooking your way around the web, using Facebook to contact and communicate is here to stay. The smart devices to me represent a major change in how and where this contact info lies. I noticed recently in my Android phone that I can sync my contacts with Gmail and/or T-Mobile so I don't lose it. I guess in the near future some of these mechanisms may cross paths either through mergers, acquisitions or just a central control system, like the old phone company. Alas Big Data is born! Long live the king… Big Data is one step from big brother!

Our Decreasing Need To Remember Anything Is Now Built In!

Of all the things I have written about in the past couple years, the decreasing need to have to remember most anything, because of the efficiencies of technology, has been one of those things that I not only think about, but live every day.

In fact we all do. When was the last time that you had to memorize a new phone number? How many email addresses do you know by heart? In fact do you find that you used to know them all by heart, but as time passes and technology changes we need to know less and less. How many times have you emailed or Text/SMS somebody asking for their mailing address and then fumbled around in Gmail looking for that email so you can buy them a gift! This trend and the ensuing impact on our lives is what I had touched on in this section of my book. And the reason

I was saying that is my involvement in 2012 to 2013 with a start-up called Connect Address.

Connect Address

Around the time I wrote a blog article on this subject, I had just started to work as a consultant with a small group in Boca Raton, Florida that was trying to find a business model. That is like saying a play in search of a playwright (That's a reference to the theater of the absurd) That start-up had already developed a Facebook store and a bunch of great technology. Their issue at the time was they did not have a serious direction. Their Facebook store really did not have a great brand, great products or a way to make revenue, less a profit. It was a dead-end. Over the next few months after meeting the owners, we changed the direction of that business from being an online retailer to being a technology company.

The trend or piece I observed within their technology, or the turning point, was when I recognized something different in their process that would be of great value to other players in the market. They had put together a process to allow a buyer on Facebook to purchase without having to know the shipping address of the recipient. The process would send a message off to the receiver and ask for a shipping address, providing a form to enter the address where they would like the product shipped.

Seeds of Not Having To Know Anything

Well, the ability to order without knowing where the order would be shipped intrigued me. A few months later I began writing my first blog post about what we can call "address-less" shipping. And when we went to the first fortune 500 company to pitch this concept, their answer was Wow, that is different, and yes we want it. So, within a few months there was a prototype app and Connect Address has been on their way since. That app has been improving and changing over the past 2 years, but the concept is pretty much the same. You are buying a gift for somebody and you don't know where they live, so you use this third party service to get it. So where does the not having to know anything come into play. Well, if you are using this new, disruptive service, you will notice that you simply login to Facebook, Twitter, Linkedin, Gmail, Yahoo and get access to your "friends". Most of their technology requires you to click on a picture to choose who you are sending the gift. End result, address-less shipping, without the pain of having to send an email off to your gift recipient, waiting for the address, keeping two browser windows open and then copy and pasting 7 times…

The History

I realize this is not just a one off event that turned into a product. Address-less, Phone-less trends are a product of the evolution of technology. I was able to trace this decreasing need to know anything trend back to the original speed dial. It was innovative at the time. Store a phone number and then just click a button. Many old phones used to have that little piece of paper you would stick in the phone that would say the name. Then it got better and better until virtual phone systems appeared. The cell phone network introduced both on board address books and voice activated address book look-up and dialing. Then Gmail (that is one I remember) introduced a bit of AI (Artificial Intelligence, which are often now just

JQuery lookups), that figures out from the few letters you have typed in what the "email" possibilities are; basically what we are going to think of next… So, cool stuff. Life is better. Now, people don't own address books anymore. Now people don't need to know your phone number. Everything is becoming built-in.

Built-Ins

So, just like your cabinets in your living room that are part of the walls, the information that connects us is built-in to the technology. Soon the next couple generations will not even know what a phone number is. Maybe they will just bump or square you and it will move from phone to phone, stored somewhere far off in a cloud server.

Google Glass And Beyond

I am not one of the 8,000 chosen to test Google Glass (Irreverently spelled, but obviously about eye glasses), but let's just say it is the next step in this evolution. With everything not having to be remembered, improving upon how you can easily access that information is the next step of this evolution. Google Glass seems to work great and I saw a user who was very happy with them. As far as Connect Address, they are still just getting started in a brave new world of helping you to not having to know one more thing, the shipping address of who you are buying a gift. It's Built In.

Thinking Like A Start-Up

Web Product Management

Measure Everything.

DIGITAL FEATURE DISCOVERY

I am not "yet" an expert on web features or product management! And I don't profess to know something that anybody else with some reasonable time on their hands, couldn't figure out. Why do I say this now? Because you have to start this way to be successful with developing web features. You have to create a clean slate in your mind, be a newbie to your project, and not be influenced by your past experience.

The Digital Feature Discovery Process

I am somewhat obsessed with the website "feature" development process, especially when it comes to overlooked, under-estimated, misused assets. This section is about how I go about discovering website features, services and solutions. We use these website assets to increase website traffic as well as finding new profitable directions, increasing conversion rates and make sites better! I am going to give a few examples, mainly from my experience working on a site like Whois.net (which is far from maximized; as far as I know they have just started the process). But first, before I describe the process to develop these features and new products (aka, the old product management process in a new era), we have to understand the lexicon of the Digital Feature Discovery process

Assets

Assets are virtual and sometimes physical things that a company owns and manages. Examples are domain names, websites, email addresses, segment or user interests, unique site visitors, page views, SMS (text), twitter accounts, Facebook and LinkedIn, Persona of the visitors (how can we break up the kinds of visitors based on background), programs and applications, patents, copyrights and internal resources like people. Oh yes, even people are assets. All these assets have a certain value and if you don't put a value on them, you are making a big mistake.

You need to start this process by working with asset value and not revenue necessarily, because while most everything in marketing is revenue based, the overall value of what you are building towards (ultimately revenue) may be determined by the long term value. On the other hand I tell start-ups I meet with that they need to go for revenue immediately in order to survive. Long term all web properties are building assets.

> "When Someone Says They Are Not Doing It For The Money, Then They Are Really Doing It For The Money"
>
> Unknown MBA Professor

Ultimately assets may determine long and even short term revenue of a website. You need to make money today, but you are building assets along the way. When I was involved in our first successful speed dating business I kept thinking if we only got to 10,000 email addresses we would be worth about $100k. Then once we get to 100,000 email addresses we would be worth about $1,000,000. In my mind I was focused on the milestone of the assets. When I would have these conversations about assets with corporate managers, they would often give me a blank stare, like they have no clue what I am talking about.

Do you know how many active email addresses your company or start-up owns?

The second thing to know about these virtual assets is the more detail you know and the more they are optimized, the more valuable are these assets. Often a firm may be collecting email addresses, but if they knew 10 additional things about these emails (people), what they were interested in, the asset value of the list may be double or triple in value. More detail like age, location, interests and salary further increase the asset value.

How do you value these assets?

My way of valuing them is simple. If you were to take them away and wanted to get them back, how much would it cost you? For instance I am going to use Whois.net, as an example. The site got about 2 million unique visits a month when I was last in charge of the site for a certain hosting company for a couple years. The company overall did not assign a serious asset value to whois.net. However, when I asked execs how much would it cost us to buy 2 million click-thrus a month by buying the PPC words "Domain Name" and "Hosting", it would have cost them a minimum $2 million dollars a month and therefor, just the traffic was worth $24 million a year or $72 million over 3 years.

It is a bit fuzzy math, but going with "take it away and try to reacquire it", is a great way to get them to understand. The reason most don't understand is they typically don't sell assets and are graded on revenue…but is that really what this is all about. If you make something worth millions maybe the asset sales is bigger than any revenue you would ever be able to generate.

So start the process by doing an inventory of assets. First day on the job and you want to make a new web feature happen at your web company, start by finding out the basics. What domains do we own? What websites do we run? What is the total number of email addresses? How many visitors to each site? How many segments are we catching from customers? How many members? How many orders? How many skus? How Many? What? Where? Why and How? Get this information down on paper, because this information is the foundation for new and improved services.

Champions

Leaders, execs, people who have an idea, guys in the company basement, and people on the customer service lines, MBAs with a business plan or just a lonely CEO with an idea are champions of web features. This means that somebody has to believe in improvements and change and wants to make it happen. A group of people may want the features to happen, but a person has to ultimately stand up and say I am a product champion. There could be many. But there has to be at least one!

Groups don't champion stuff, individuals do. This is one of the critical mistakes made by corporations and some start-ups, to think that a group of people will decide by committee ultimately what a web feature will do and how it goes is a big mistake. Sometimes web features are made by a dictator. If the champion is a dictator, he may have a chance if he is a benevolent dictator and listens well and adopts ideas and suggestions by anybody who can contribute to the project.

An entrepreneurial environment is what works best, even in a big corporation. Funny thing is this champion cannot be limited to execs with great salaries and titles like VP, Director, CEO, CIO, CTO, BFD or Founder. A champion can and should be anybody. That is what makes companies succeed, not a special group who can only do the thinking. It can and should by anyone. Champions need support and guidance and promoters from above, below and sideways. Being a champion has its risks as I've learned. You can get burned by being the champion. But you can also have amazing success. It is not about the accolades, it's about making something happen.

Little Trees

Years ago we used to pay to plant trees in Israel. And then years later when I visited Israel I got a chance to see those trees grow. In order to grow a tree in the future, a big tree, you have to plant seedlings or small trees today. This is where many execs lose their patience and understanding of the product management process. You have to test, test and test again these little trees in order to find a big one. Ok, if you don't get the tree allegory of ideas, you may be missing the point. Where do you find these little "seedling" ideas? There everywhere.

Somebody recently said, "Dan's An Idea Guy!" That is not true. I am not an idea guy, I am a guy who listens and hears other people's concepts and evolves them into ideas. There are ideas all around us, if we would take the time to just listen and sort through the data. Remember, the assets… Just doing an inventory will start to flesh out these little trees or concepts or ideas. One thing I always did at these companies is walk around and chat with the various people in the business. They have ideas. They know what may or may not work and though they don't know how to implement, they do know something they are not telling everybody. Often it's something in the business that bugged them for years that they want to share.

Sharing

Never thought the Digital Feature Discovery process would come down to sharing, but learning to share, something my 4 year old has not yet mastered, is the key way towards finding those little trees. People need to get together and chat and think and find answers. These answers are something somebody read somewhere. A company environment where people don't share their thoughts is a place that will never flesh out new concepts or web features. Look at Google, they are actually asking for the ideas and look what they have produced. If we want the rest of corporate America to be successful on the web, they better listen up and start to share. Like I said earlier, it is the champion that takes an idea and makes sure it happens, not the product management guy or gal. The product management person should be the facilitator and not the creator in the end. Listen and learn, not ignore and complain. Sometimes doing your job requires less, not more of giving and taking. Learn the small lessons from your childhood like I am teaching my son and share. The secret to sharing is giving of oneself. If you cannot give to others, by give I mean tell people something about yourself or your ideas, you will not be able to acquire ideas. The sharing has to start with you.

The Other Guys

The easiest way to find a niche and the things that people have not thought of and get the real brainstorm going on is by knowing what is happening in the market. You actually need to go off and look carefully at the competitors. This is not about mimicking people. This is about concept development. You see a feature on another competitor and you grab it. Fine, but you not only have to take it, you have to own it and therefor it needs to come from your mind and recreated in a new way. What I ended up doing for my Whois.net thesis for my MBA is reading through 500 similar websites. From this exercise alone I ended up with a dozen new products and features for the Whois.net site.

No rocket science involved here. It is simply looking and learning.

Integrative Strategic Thinking (Aha Moments)

Once you have all this data in front of you, the assets, new ideas and the competitive information, you can now start to mash things together to produce something new. This should produce new concepts from a higher perspective. At this higher level, as you look holistically at information. You can start to piece together stuff you did not see originally in the assets alone. For instance, when I looked through and discovered that Whois.net did not allow international domain name look-ups, I knew immediately this was an important issue. The importance was simple enough. If you increase upon (extend) what people already like, you will probably have success. They used to call it product extensions. This is where you take a product that is already successful and you add on a new feature or extend the product to new areas. Not a high risk activity. For Whois.net, international domain name traffic look-ups blew out the traffic, automatically doubling site traffic in six months and it tripled and quadrupled traffic over a year. Just satisfying people with stuff they already wanted is easy. However, what is easy to do, is often difficult to see by management with blindfolds on. And when you are busy in a high end corporate product management job, you are blinded by the requests from above and from the sides.

Stats and Prioritization

What did I do with the 500 websites I viewed in my thesis on Whois searches? I came up with a scientific approach to figure out what feature was important. Most of you who read this probably prioritize every day. I rated each feature by value (yes a monetary value), ease of implementation, where I found it, as well as the monetary value of the websites I reviewed. This review process was not about money, it was about assets again. What I focused on was how do I get visitors to this site, not on how do I convert? I was leaving conversion and selling at this point up to marketing and sales. That was something they knew how to do pretty well. What you need to as a good champion is to understand the data beneath the hood and how to use this data to make a point. Prioritization and hitting low hanging fruit are extremely important ways of working as well. We are in an impatient world, where execs don't have the time or energy to listen unless they are just seeing the cream of the crop. Maybe they shouldn't know everything till the time is right. Sometimes companies kill a product or project the first time around because it failed. That does not mean the second time it will be the same.

Learn From Mistakes, Don't Bury Them

Organizations that learn from their mistakes and take actions the second time around to make things right are rare. Most organizations bury a concept that has failed and when it is mentioned again by a newbie, the newbie is crushed with the notion that "this has failed here". This is a big mistake. Failure should never be viewed as a doorway an organization cannot go through again. It should, however, be the shining example of how not to do the same thing, the same way. Failure should be used as a way to understand what to do right next time. Like a pyramid, building upon their knowledge, great organizations store this learned mistake information and use it positively going forward.

Leapfrog

One of the concepts I learned while working on a well ignored site like Whois.net was if you are so far behind the competition, it is sometimes worth it, to not mimic, but rather take a leap of faith and go for something greater, different, in a way that competitors would never do. Why won't they? The competitor has already made their product or web feature decision and taken the current path. If they are leaders in the market already, it will take a lot for them to change. This leap of faith may be something like give it away for free, or combine it with something new or offer something completely different or in a way that is easy to identify but not the same. Simply cookie cutter mimicking is a nuisance on the web. Who wants to go to Bing, when Google does it so well? Why would I ever do that, other than Microsoft has figured out a way to trap me when I load the next IE Browser? Now if Bing did something so different, so incredibly well done, it would make sense. If Bing was better on an iPad, there would be a competitive advantage, but they are no better. If they were better with voice search that would be different. If they were better or different, it would matter! Making it matter means being different not the same. In the case of Whois.net, I was determined to make the site a competitor with Sedo.com, the domain auction house, except my idea was to make it a free place to buy and sell domains. Sedo.com is not free. This is the kind of leap that makes a difference and can have an impact on the "asset value".

Ok, so you have finally figured out the key assets and are starting to go down the road of making your new web feature happen… well let's just say you are only 20%

towards the finish line. There are some major hurdles involved for most of us, including even the big guy or gal at the top. The thinking part of discovering ripe juicy revenue or visitor producing features is the easy part. The difficult part is making it happen, navigating the human beings all along the way, especially when you know they are all trying to make sure you fail directly, fail indirectly, fail just by the fact that you don't have the energy to fight anymore, fail because you left the job or fail because the job left you. It is a fight to the death my friend and it's all because you sorted through the company assets with a flashlight at night when nobody was looking and you had an idea you brought it into the daylight. Now you are a pure unadulterated target for those who don't want you to succeed! So how do you proceed in the murkiest of environments?

Social Engineering

I first began to understand social engineering, when I was reading a great article about Kevin Mitnick, the infamous hacker who broke into Sprint and stole tons of information about their customers. He was not a genius. He was not very technical. He was basically a petty thief. How did he do it? He used social engineering. If you think about it, social engineering (in the Mitnick version) is about figuring out how to use information and people of an organization to think what you want them to think and do, using that information wisely. Mitnick figured out that when executives names where mentioned, people lose their minds and do what you want. "Uh, Leader Dick the VP said we need that report now!" Mitnick found out that if you know some small piece of information or just a name, you could easily navigate an entire organization, call around to people and they would hand you off like you were a friend and more importantly a new hire. He would use person X's name and say hey person Y, Person X recommended me. What he really did is say the VP wanted me to get onto System Z, NOW, so give me a login and password...

The point is, you need to understand the dynamics of the organization, the motivations of people in the organization and the hierarchy of decision-making. Getting the organization on board with you is what I am getting at! But ultimately, like I have said before, you can take the high road or the low road. Taking the high road means bring the organization along on a ride towards success (success means getting your feature implemented).

Education Camp

Sometimes unusual methods are needed in order to gain the trust of execs and the whole organization. For instance, some of the features I was trying to get implemented at my last company required me to make sure that the organization understood the features. What did I do about it? I ran a seminar. Now people in my company who came to my seminar looked at me oddly. Who was I to run a seminar? I was just a programmer there, sometimes a manager, but in no way did I have the keys to the kingdom or really was in charge of much there. Fellow employees would look at me with confused looks. Who was this guy standing up there talking about things? I ran periodic internal seminars at the office. This means a short 45 minute talk, on WordPress for instance. I ran a seminar on Whois. I was planning a seminar on a variety of subjects. What was I doing in my crazy convoluted method was starting the social engineering process by planting seeds through my seminars. I wanted this company to adopt certain strategies and methods. Once again, nobody stopped me from running a talk at noon time in the conference rooms. This is a great place to flesh out your ideas and don't freak if someone shows up to show you up. My answer to them would be, show me how to do it better!

Plan 32 And The Road Always Taken

One thing that a great web product manager should always have is a pile of ready to go plans in their back pocket. You have all the plans (I mean PPTs, Power Points) that are company planned, on the so called "Road Map". Actually I am going to digress here and tell you that if somebody in a company tells you on the first day there is a Road Map, beware of the kind of situation where nothing can be accomplished! The kind of process and thinking a Road Map can create can be a real negative, because from experience nay-sayers love to use the Road Map as a way to block new "Road Entrances". Never let the Road Map to be used as a "Weapon" to keep critical processes from being re-prioritized and redeveloped. I have yet to see the Road Map (in the web feature world) be the best guide. Now, as far as plans are concerned, you have the top line plans already planned out from the execs and board. You have the plans that others know about that you are promoting. You have a dozen others that they are not aware of. You have them ready to go, in standby mode, in a file on your hard-drive or cloud, just in case the time is right. Why the three types of plans? Well, part of succeeding is not giving it all away too soon. You have to release plans periodically to the organization, who can't handle all the plans at once. They have to be part of a series of changes over time. Once again, as a champion, of a lot of other people's ideas (OPIs), you need to map out these features properly and get your presentations just right. Sometimes you have to sit on things and let osmosis occur. You wake up one morning and your brain somehow figures it out. Who knows why things work that way, but often they do. I would highly recommend sitting down with all the guys and gals who thought of the original concept and show them where their idea is now!

The Shadow Government

Sometimes all the education and all the presentations and all the board room brawls are insignificant compared with the reality that something has to be done subversively. It is a rare thing to do, and there are some well documented cases where it is a necessity. A great example is the case of the James Cannavino at IBM. I read a great story about Jim in the late 1960s trying to convince management that he could speed up the IBM Mainframe. They rejected his notion, but in a subversive move, he had the technology developed outside the company in his home garage. When it was finished, he went over his bosses heads and showed it to the board. He faced either being fired or being promoted. Luckily he was promoted. Hopefully it doesn't come to this, but sometimes getting things done in an organization require unusual activity, because like I have been inferring there are many more forces at work trying to not make things happen than happen, even on the smallest scale.

Project Mercury

Those funny project names often mimicking Nasa projects are not just wild imaginative words that are spread around at a company. They are used to get your attention, to try to get the organization to recognize a plan. These project names may sound strange and odd, but motivate your partners, employees and even your customers, even in a start-up. Twitter and LinkedIn and Facebook are now household names, but 15 years ago they would sound strange. And it is only going to get stranger. When I say Tweet, Joomla, Droopal, lamp or soap to people in the web world; they better know what I mean… What should be happening in most American web firms is an injection of militarization combined with humor and something to spice it up. That's what a project name is all about. If project names are not attention-getters, they are the wrong names. I would always try to make the name relevant, but a good bit of creativity is a positive not a negative.

Misdirection And The Book Of 5 Rings

Talking about military tactics, people's military training can go a long way in corporate America. Just because I was not in the army, doesn't mean we can't learn from military tactics. They are important. At the end of my MBA program I took a class which revolved around Musashi's *The Book Of Five Rings*. Musashi is a Japanese expert on war in the middle ages who survived to his old age. Because Musashi was one of the few warriors to survive, he knew he had knowledge and tactics that he had used to gain a long life. One of the tactics listed is a method of drawing an enemy towards oneself and at the last minute let the enemy run themselves off a cliff. In our language we call it misdirection. Sometimes you have to lead people down a path and not stop them from their self-destruction. Often your plan has one way of doing things and another person has their plan. If you see their plan is faulty you don't always have to stop it from failing. Sometimes it is best to let it fail. When I worked back at the phone company we used to leave documents around about projects that were never in existence in order to confuse people about what our real intentions were. Sometimes it is important to not reveal these intentions until you are ready to make it happen.

Start With The End In Mind

So in digital feature discovery, I have described identifying assets and dealing with people, the two ingredients needed to build any web site feature. Who knew these were important to building a website! The next step is information discovery. Assets need to be understood and evaluated in an open and free environment, not restricted by management that has already indicated the final outcome. Knowing the exact, final website product on day one is ok as a goal, but to know the exact way it will work is a not just a mistake, it can create a terrible work environment for those who see the mistakes and can't fix them. You start with a general idea of where you want to go in development of web features, and great spec's (short for specification) can make this possible. There is a transformation that needs to occur between concept and final product. That is where a lot of websites go awry by simply never fixing what needs to be fixed.

Information Discovery

Information discovery is all about looking through the data, which leads to idea discovery. But even before you go through reams of data, you need to figure out what you are trying to accomplish. This is a bit of a conundrum, like which came first the chicken or the egg. Let's say you have a web page or a web site that is already doing its job. Your site could be a simple page or 2 or be as large as a 20,000 SKU online catalog. I've built both sites in the past. The question is how do you figure out that you need to add a form to collect information or to place ads on the site? How do you know if the site should be a marketplace or a straight e-commerce site? This is not just about data. This is about business and business models. If you have worked on developing websites you probably know a thing or 2 about making your own website.

In the first part of digital feature discovery, I described assets and where you have to look for key information. Are there any anomalies showing a possible opportunity, or as Google in their web analytics product calls it, Intelligence? Is this site getting tremendous numbers of visitors? Is this site already collecting email addresses? One site I know of, because I am a part owner, gets an email address added to the system every 10 minutes during the day. This asset is important, because email addresses can be, should be used properly. By properly, I mean when people give you an email address, they are expecting an immediate response. The value of the email starts to go down when you wait 6 months till you email them. The fresher, the more valuable, and that's because people have a small period of time to read that email you will send them. This has led to the concept of email sequences. First time I had heard about this was from my business partner, who pointed out a company called Infusionsoft, which made sequencing their bread and butter. It's really a simple concept. You have a series of emails that get sent out to a person that signs up, which is sent in a sequential time frame like once a day, once a week, perhaps growing in length of time. Each email has a different message that is part of an overall strategy. You don't need Infusionsoft to do this, but they are great at it.

Let The Wind Tell You Where To Go

Often data is telling you something. For instance, on Whois.net, we noticed a high amount of international visitors, yet we did not offer the ability to look up international domains. So we solved the customer's quandary by offering what they were looking for. So one clue is looking at the key words people search on to get to your site in Google Analytics or Adobe's/Omniture's Site Catalyst. This is a simple task and 90% of online marketers should know this. What they don't look for is the missing link. The missing piece is what ties information to a new potential set of features. Another good example is on checkout of most registration sites, there is a term we now call "Co-registration". Co-registration means the customer was here to sign up for x, and you added another potential thing for them to get at the same time. We have considered using this in the event business website I am a partner in. Another interesting anomaly I noticed in the dating business recently is that people are using iPhones and Android apps to signup, in significant numbers. This is where you have to brain-storm, not about features, but about assumptions. You can confirm these assumptions, through research. My assumption that people are using smartphones, specifically at work during the day is because it offers more privacy, and the employer can't track you specifically. This is one of many reasons. The end result is we need to have a mobile-ready website and possibly a mobile app for the iPhone and Android... That is simple detective work.

This is the big breakthrough. It is finding a new channel. The big question is having the resources to capitalize on this new channel. It may not be a new channel to you, but to a lot of executives out there, who don't know how to deal with this channel, it is a strange new world. The next channel we are seeing is both Wearable Computer and Google Glass. They are new channels that will be served in new ways.

In the retail side we use Cross-Sell or Up-Sell. You will get a complete lesson on up-sell and cross-sell by signing up for Godaddy. Godaddy is the masters of cross-sell! I used to have people say what Godaddy does lead to Friction, one of the key points in the MarketingExperiments.com formula, where it will actually causes less conversion potentially. This all depends on the site and business model. On a dating site, yes, too much Friction can slow the process down, especially if the person is not ready to convert. On a retail site, however, when people have made up their minds to buy, only a broken, poorly designed web page can stop them, especially if the deal is an amazingly good value. So most features are figured out as extensions of what you already have in place. If you build on your success, you will succeed even more. There is no need to take big risks. Most product extensions and improvements are simply improving upon what you already have.

Slash And Burn

If you let the status quo dictate what you do, or worse, let the current sales and marketing team make *all* the decisions, you could end up with a situation I call "slash and burn". I came across the concept of slash and burn, while working on a few sites. The analogy of slash and burn comes from the military tactic of burning the crops as you retreat, so your enemy will not have the luxury of food. It refers to the, sometimes unforeseen, consequences of making a decision to kill one part of a website in order to enhance another. This is a human decision process, typically driven by personal objectives. The best example was on this Whois.net site, where, when I arrived at this company, the previous manager, who managed Whois.net, had attempted to drive all the traffic through links on the site to hosting sales on another site, because that is where the money was for them and their group. This was a major mistake in my mind. Yes, they had driven people to where they could make money, but that is not why they came to Whois.net. They were there to look up domains that were available, find out who owns them, and buy domains if they were available.

Consistency

Another very important point is consistency in the process of building out web features. I will discuss them a lot here. You have to start at the beginning of the customer path. A start or beginning is when the customer or user is sitting at their computer on an Ipad. Let's say they have not even turned it on. They are interested in South Florida Real Estate, as an example. They open the computer and type "South Florida Real Estate" into Google. Google presents them with relevant results. Let's say your site is in those results. When you click on one of the links, and let's say it's one of the top paid links, you are delivered to a web page. The words you searched for should arrive right in your face at the top of the webpage you have arrived at in big bold letters. If not, you are not getting a consistent experience. This is consistently not true for many paid links. That's because they are using something called Long Tail, which has a few meanings. To me, it means extending the search words they are buying out to more obscure or more specific words, to pay less and get more traffic. This would typically mean they are looking to buy "Real Estate", but it was cheaper to buy "South Florida Real Estate". This is great for smaller sites and pages that are meant to be found locally, but when you arrive at a generic Real Estate Seminar, which is not what you were looking for, you are disappointed. This is not Google's fault, it's about people trying to get traffic, and the result is a lot of inconsistency. Your consistency is critical in making your site found well and sticky, a term these marketing guys love to use (meaning they stick around).

Don't Make Me Think Even More

I mention *Don't Make Me Think* several times in this book. If you work in the web field, you should get it today, read it, and live by it. You need to make sure the customer experience is not so different from what they expect, that they exit the website. From the web features perspective, deliver to customers at least the minimum they are expecting on the site. More and more, customers are expecting a web form (to leave their email) on the home page and sometimes many site pages, where they can put their email address in, maybe with their first name or some additional data and get on that companies' mailing list. When there is not email box to leave your contact info, many times you are missing out on a big opportunity. If you do not support Facebook login, maybe it is time!

Each technology highway has a logical end. The question is will you take an exit before the highway ends.

PIVOTING A START-UP: HOW TO AVOID THE BIG DISASTER

As one unnamed CEO of an NTT Corp division told me,

> "I have seen more disasters in my lifetime. This is looking like a disaster. Let's try to avoid a big disaster on this one!"

Commitment To Failure

A few years ago in my MBA program at Florida Atlantic University (FAU) I remember studying the concept of Commitment To Failure. This is when a business has chosen a strategic initiative where they are going to finish the project or literally die as a business. It's often an ego thing and the company doesn't want to lose the time spent on a project, even if it is going nowhere. But you have to lose sometimes to gain. In extreme cases executives or business owners make a choice to hit a target or go out of business. They typically don't talk about it this way and denial is part of the issue. Somewhere in the back of their mind there is a chance that they will not make it. Everybody knows that is the risk of business. But why go out of business when you could have stopped or changed direction or made an adjustment and survived.

The Strength Of The Human Mind

Someone recently told me about a strong willed businessman he met with who dominated the conversation at a business lunch meeting with this person. This web development consultant had started a contract with a small business owner who would not let him talk, and shut him down if he opened his mouth with a never ending barrage of words. While at lunch the consultant was not allowed to look at the menu. The guy demanded he look at him and listen and controlled everything. The megalomaniac, smartest guy in the room syndrome, is the one you have to spot right away. I often joke that these are the guys or gals who sometimes make millions because of their crazy ways, but on the other hand they kill themselves with their all-knowing, god-like complexes. Hope you haven't had the opportunity to work with this kind of person. They make life difficult for everybody for no reason. And it doesn't have to be that way.

The Inevitable Future

I love this book *Inevitable Surprises* by Peter Schwartz, where he tells us that the seeds of the future are always around us in the data. We can see through a crystal ball if we really want to. I highly recommend this book if you are trying to figure out new trends for your start-up. Once the future hits and something becomes a reality we are always surprised, but the tea leaves were always there. People sit around now and say the mortgage industry collapsed for instance, but most of us remember the housing bubble, the 40 and 50 year mortgages, the no questions asked mortgage and lots of other programs that were obviously going to sink the housing business in 2007. These red herrings were right in front of us and the future was something you could sense. Often we see all the signs but we ignore them. I have.

Stop, Drop And Roll

So why be ignorant about your own start-up and make the right change early, not when the business is on the ropes? Great companies have done this and pulled themselves in a new direction. It's a rarity, but it happens. Look at Bill Gates in 1995 in the wee hours realizing that the Internet is big and waking up and changing his company direction in the morning! It does not matter how big the company is, sometimes you have to change directions and give up on an idealistic trend that did not make sense. Can you take what you have already created and go in a new direction, or do you have to start over from scratch? It depends. Is your start-up or business division doomed to failure down the road? Then start a new direction, now, not when the start-up or division has been laid to rest. Great businesses know when to say no to a project and either stop or switch gears. A good example I am going through right now is taking my Take It National software project. I had to make a decision this it is not heading in a good direction and stop.

First Success Syndrome

One particular syndrome I have notice for start-up guys and gals who have hit the big one the first time around is First Success Syndrome. Just because they were 23 and created Facebook, they think they now know everything they need to know in life. This is the kind of person that typically makes the commitment to failure the second and third times around. I hear a lot about 2nd time failures and many failures for first time successes. Why does this happen? I guess our minds play a trick on us and we end up thinking that we know what we are doing and we stop listening. I would say listening and looking at information can tell you there is a problem and there is a failure coming down the line. For instance when any young entrepreneur tells me that he is going to create a new non-profit and will make tons of money, I look at him and say "No, not going to happen". Non-profits should generally not make you rich. They can, but then I would say something unusual is happening. Generally speaking it does not sound kosher.

The 911 Here

Like I said, I don't know everything. I think that is the first attitude you need in looking at your business, your business division and any business situation. Listening to people is the key to success and not knowing everything!

Sorting Out What's Important

Years ago, those of us who worked for Bell Atlantic in the 90s, went to a management training program called The Bell Atlantic Way. The Way was one of a dozen management training programs we were sent through.

Management training was in vogue back then and the phone company was still transitioning from the old guard to the new guard. This just means that the old time phone company employees were being brought along and lead into the brave new world of cellular and other new technologies like the Internet. The company feared that the employees were not really prepared for this change. They were the old time operating phone company employees. In fact one lady, Elsie, had her 50th anniversary of work for good old Bell in my group. Her first job was teaching people the rotary dial! But I was not one of the old timers. I was in my mid-20s, but I attended these brain changing management programs as well.

There was a Quality Training program and other programs that we went through. It seemed like there was one every 6 months. The one that stuck in my mind and still does was The Way. Most of us who attended The Way seminars probably still remember the core points. In particular the one lesson that I remember the most was Blue Chips, Red Chips and Yellow Chips. What they were trying to teach us is that we needed to look over all our chips, work tasks, and make a determination of which color each task or chip represented. Important ones got a Blue chip, Red for medium and Yellow for chips that could wait. We would need to reorganize our priorities based on the Blue Chips. It sounds simple for most of us. But for engineers (and almost everybody at the phone company was an engineer) it is not possible to always prioritize on what is really important. In fact I have seen many engineers focus on minutiae and details that are not important to the overall business.

Fast forward 20 years. Seems like many of the Internet

start-up guys did not need to learn this blue chip lesson. They figured a lot out on their own. But let's just say that for every successful tech start-up there are something like 3 or more that don't make it. Why? Because (trust me on this) they may have been thinking like an engineer and not a business person. What was important was getting to critical mass or revenue compared with making something cool. Now there is a second part of this, a conundrum. What is quite ironic is the cool technologies make the big bucks in the end! For many start-ups having Google Engineers and amazing technology is quite important. For some all this talk about what is important from a business stand-point may not matter. But when you are an Internet start-up out there in small town in America or overseas and not in Silicon Valley, NYC, Chicago, Boston or Austin, you pretty much have to figure out what is important.

So, let's say you are in a start-up and you partner with a technology guy or gal. Please make sure that you don't let them drive the business. If you are in charge, and you want to succeed and you wrote the business plan, don't let it go in a different direction. It is important, as long as you are quite sure about your target, that you don't let technology people drive the business into the ground. They may become consumed with small details that is not critical. It happens to me all the time. And it even happens when I take on the role as developer. Sometimes I build some additional code that was not necessary.

Thinking can be a problem for the technology mind. Sometimes you have to close down your creative mind and just do what you are told if you are not driving the bus! The real definition of a programmer is a person who does what they are told to do exactly!

Dan Gudema

Simplify, Simplify Again, and Simplify a 3rd time.

John Kemp

FEATURE OVERLOAD IN WEB PRODUCT MANAGEMENT

Having come into contact with at least 20 different websites and start-ups over the past 2 months, plus having to manage all the features in our new start-up Krowde, I am starting to see the light on the words "Simplify, Simply Again, and Simply a 3rd time". Back when we were at Caffeine Spaces in Boca Raton, someone wrote this quote from John Kemp on the dry erase board. It has a lot of meaning to me and can be applied to so many aspects of building out a website or mobile app from design, functionality, marketing, architecture and other aspects of these tech startups. I am focused on product management in this context. (but I it could apply to any of those disciplines)

Feature Junkie

Simplification has a lot of meaning to me because I am a feature junkie. Every time I come up with a new product or concept, I can think of a million cool features. This is what we do as creative people. When you combine that with a technologist, more specifically a web developer, you can have a thousand little features that are cool and different and meant to change the world, even a world within a world. But overall, what you are doing with complexity sometimes is really showing off your ego. We all want to show off what we can do and how smart we are. Generally we are very smart, but not always in business. Trust me, it's my downfall. In web product management too many features and quite often the wrong features can be the death of a product or at least delay it indefinitely before it goes live.

What's The Delay And I Want It All Now!

Now, if you think about it, how can you produce all these features when your time is limited? That is not the real question. The real question is what features are really needed first, and what features can't wait. I can't really expound on the features in Krowde that I am talking about, but I can come up with an imaginary app that I probably will never create. Let's call it Park Finder, and let's say it was being built for iOS and Android.

You have spec'd out the mobile app for Park Finder. You have come up with a dozen great features like

- a map with icons
- a search of that map

- a link to that park's page
- a listing and a small profile per park
- the ability to share that Park with your friends instantly via Facebook, Linkedin, Twitter
- an ability to talk about that park
- an ability to upload pictures about that park for others to see
- rate that park
- a list of parks by ratings
- park contact info
- park office instant chat

Wait a second! That last one needs to go into the list of "Would Like" stuff. And that is the issue. In fact, this list has a lot of cool stuff, but ultimately this park finder app could actually be live and working with just 3 features, a search, a map and a link to the website for that park. All the other park finder features sound so good in your head and they are, but the customers don't know what they don't know!

Customers Don't Know What They Don't Know

I like saying this line "Customers Don't Know What They Don't Know" because it is really important and tied to the simplification concept. The second issue with product complexity occurs in the mind of the technology founder. Sometimes they think that more is better. They think that the value increases with number and breadth of features. But it is not exactly the same for the customer or customers. Customers don't always think the same or use the same features. When only 5 out of 1000 users used that feature then of course it was not very important. Also, from a development standpoint, what about getting the thing finished and out to the market. That is what is critically important!

Timing

Getting the Park app out into the market, with limited features is the best way to do it. It is what Fried says in *Rework*, Brad Feld says in his blog and it makes common sense. If you want to get your product out there and in the market, only include at first the core features, the features that make your product usable. It will not fail because it does not have all the final pieces and bells and whistles you envision. It may be that the park finder app may have been well received and done very well with only these basic features. You have the time to add new features after that. Add your sharing, commenting, rating and other features later on. It is painful but worth it and the difference in your app making or not making it to market.

What Can I Live Without?

In the end people are the problem, because even I have fallen into the "I want it all" trap. And then I was the problem. You think you can have it all, but sometimes more doesn't necessarily sell your product. Sometimes less does. Sometimes doing a small thing well is more critical than anything. There are products and services that are bigger and feature rich, but they are not for the small boot strapped start-up. There is a cost associated with more and sometimes those features never amount to anything or any usage. Management and people you can't always control. They may be in charge and have decision making and the purse strings. But at least you understand yourself what the issues are, and can say to yourself, what can I live without?

Thinking Like A Start-Up

Web People

I start with the premise that I don't know the answer to anything, truly!

HOW TO RESPOND TO NEW IDEAS?

Recently I had to remind a few people, after covering a new concept that my team wants to try, that we are "old" guys and that we really may not know much of anything when it comes to deciding what is a good idea or bad idea. Let me first preface the word "idea". When I refer to an "idea" in the Internet space we are mainly referring to a new business, a new website, a new mobile app, hardware, a new start-up company, or a new conceptual technology thingy that actually does something. Actually the words he used were "But I know what I like". And those words to me mean very little because what we like or think we like may only lead us to a big mistake. Trust me, what we like will not exactly work for everybody, or even a small group of the mass market. There are a lot of things I like technically in life. I still like my old PC I am working on right now. I have a MacBook Pro next to it. I don't like it. But who am I to say what I like is what everybody likes.

What WE LIKE May Not Mean Anything

To work with entrepreneurs with new ideas, you have to leave your ego at the door and be an open book. So a few weeks earlier a young entrepreneur with a new concept wanted to sit with me and discuss his new Web & Mobile App. After hearing his pitch I sat thinking to myself, "Wow, this is a dumb idea, this marketing plan won't work, and this logo and business name does not work for me." So what did I do? I sat there and just bit my tongue. Just because I think it is bad or wrong, does not mean I am correct. I may be right, but it may not matter. The question is how to dish out the mentoring and get them to a point that you are helping and not being a jerk.

The Weekly Meet-up & Mentoring

At least once a week an entrepreneur or a person I met at DSX Labs wanted to sit with me and discuss their app. It may be just a concept not yet on paper, or a full blown application especially if it is in the Dating space, Social Networking, Education Space or areas I have been exposed to. I always take the meeting. And I have to force myself to sit and listen. This is not easy, because those who know me, know that I have a bad habit of interjecting "cutting people off" when they are talking and just start saying my own ideas.

I have to STOP and focus and buckle down to get the gist of what they are trying to get across. Listening is really mentoring. Giving some rational tactical advice on Next

Steps is the answer. Every tech entrepreneur is in a certain stage of development. If they don't have their one page Exec Summary or a Pitch Deck, that is where they need to do next. This is especially true if they want to raise capital or just bring on partners or customers.

Small Steady Improvements

Conceptually any idea can be developed into a lasting entity or business, especially if the concept is tested. This friend of mine had this one business venture we talked about where he had failed to gain critical mass, and we discussed a little bit of why it failed. He felt his "vision" had not been accepted by the market. I think I made a very simple point. He should have tested the market better and determined earlier what would work and what would not work. You can spend very little to throw together a cheap website or survey to find out some information that would help determine if the market exists. Even then, we can be wrong and have received wrong signals from the market. The point is, he should have tested the concept and broken it down into small pieces and gotten a web page up and running and just made small improvements finding his way towards success. That is how you have to approach this business.

> "Investing in the Internet is similar in a way to investing in a farm"
>
> Yossi Vardi

Read this great quote by Israeli technology pioneer Yossi Vardi. Essentially you have to look at Internet related ventures like you do farming. I have to remind all the people I meet with new ideas to think like this and to sell them this way. 90% of the results of our Internet ventures will take 3-5 years to show results. And of that amount, many may fail, but many will succeed if you continue to make improvements and pivot and figure out how to get to market and make revenue. Everything takes a lot longer to happen. Start-ups that seem like overnight successes, sometimes had to fail several times before figuring out how to succeed.

Dan Gudema

An IT person in charge means an inmate may be running the asylum.

MANAGING THE IT PERSON

One of the quirkiest and hard to explain things in this world is the mind of the IT person. If that person is a programmer, they can be off the charts crazy. That could be crazy in a good way or crazy in a bad way. It could mean a crazy good programmer. There are all kinds of people in this world. People in the IT profession don't just run the gamut, they can be perfect gentlemen or total freaks. There are all kinds of people in this world. Just happens that people who work in technology can be difficult and non-expressive at times. It even happens to me, especially when working with very difficult coding issues. IT professionals can let their inner emotions get the best of themselves and do some pretty weird things like holler, not show up, get angry over some small piece of code or technology not done right, or simply be so unable to communicate they need to go through a third person.

The Cold Techie

If you are dealing with a non-expressive personality, what we used to call an analytical person, you need to make sure you will notice that they are extremely careful and analytical in how they work with you. If you want to work with this kind of person well, then give them more time to get things accomplished and be careful to listen to them well.

The IT Social-lite

When it comes to people who like to not just work the code, web servers and iPhone internals, but also love a good joke, you are most likely dealing with a Social personality. They are not so concerned primarily with the work at hand. If you want to get their attention and work with them, always ask "how they feel" first.

Tech Educators

There is a variant of tech personality, sometimes called a promoter, which loves to listen, educate and give feedback. This is the personality I fall under, sometimes. This is the person who is sending around all the latest Tweets and posts interesting stuff on the company blog.

Vector Directors

There is one tech personality type which can be very useful in one case and in another it can cause be a major problem for your Start-Up. This is the director personality. Sometimes I ask Start-Ups if they have a difficult personality in IT or the programmer or worse a partner. If they say yes, I remind them that could be the end of their Start-Up. Yes, the personalities can end it all. If people can't work together than just stop right now.

Team Work

A Start-Up in the end is a team exercise. You can't do it all yourself. You have to enlist others or find a co-founder. The all-in-one successful Start-Up person does not exist. Even if they are the business, to succeed they had to get somebody else to work on their team.

Co-founders often work like puzzle pieces. The best teams are made up of people who have very different personalities. Working together is critical at the same time. There is a yin and a yang to co-founders. They may not get along personally, but they have to be able to get along enough to get everything necessary completed.

This is not just about small Start-Ups. Big corporations have the same issues when it comes to team work. The only exception is it is like 100 times worse than a small team. What happens in big corporate life is sometimes literally 100 people have to be involved in a new product or service online. While usually it takes about 7 team members for a website, there are other divisions, many layers of management and all kinds of people who step in and work as a team member. Just one bad apple in this bunch can cause big time trouble.

Why You Have To Be Founder & Psychologist

A Start-up IT team needs to work together harmoniously. If there are any bumps in the road, that could end the whole venture. There was one case with a Start-Up I consulted with where a person was so volatile to the entire venture, they had to stop and spend 90% of their time on trying to find a way to work with this person. What you typically see is the seeds of this person's discontent and problematic personality were there on day 1. What you have to do is look for the signs of a problem as early as possible. Can you work with this person? Will this person make life so intolerable people will quit left and right. It is sort of like a cancer you have to remove early on.

Dan Gudema

Your GMAT score is inversely related to your ability to run your own business!

LEARNING IS EARNING

A few years ago, and I would love to find this article again, on Yahoo Finance, there was an article about why you should just forget about getting an MBA. Just start an Internet start-up and skip business school! That is what the writer prescribed. Not sure if this was written to get the Yahoo Finance readers up in arms or to make a point. It did get lots of responses, good and bad. And in some ways I totally agree with the writer. In some ways I did not. I had my own answer to this, but my situation was very different than the audience the writer was writing for. It does not matter how young or old you are, more education to me is always a good thing. It may not help you with a start-up, but I personally would love to have a dozen more degrees!

I stole this line, "Your GMAT Score Is Inversely Related To Your Ability To Run Your Own Business" from a book I read years ago on how to survive the Harvard business school. Yes, it is true that MBA programs train people to work at companies and deal with big company issues. It is also true the degree is a generalist degree in many ways, kind of like an engineering degree. What you learn in school may not be useful in real life. And it may actually be true that those who go to get their business degree or MBA are often not able to start and run their own business, but when I ask entrepreneurs if they could have an MBA right now to assist them in their business; their answer is always yes. It is always better to have more education. I would get a PHD, if I had unlimited money, time and resources.

More Learning Means More Money

If you do some research you will find that the more education you get, the more you generally earn. Obviously we would all love to start a company and make money on our own working for ourselves, but the statistics say that overall getting more education means more money. It is a simple principle. Also, not everybody can go off and start an Internet company. There are as many failures in online business as there are offline. It is easier and faster to start a business online and thousands of new websites every year prove it. You can't knock people from trying, but don't argue this start-up method is an alternative to an MBA. You can have an MBA and be in a start-up, in fact that combination is more powerful than a start-up founder without an MBA.

I Went To Learn

My MBA education was not about the degree. Well, it became about finishing the degree in the last year (when I wanted to end!). Overall, it was done over time, at 2 schools and I literally took my time. I tried to use the time in class to enhance my day job. This was not about the degree, it was about my mind. I think it is important to learn and not just be handed a piece of paper. One of the issues that speak broadly about this is the lack of ethics among MBA grads. Well, if they are not about learning, and just about the degree, what do you expect them to be like? There are many people with no ethics. That's why we often hear about guys like Madoff running a scam.

Education Realization

I recently had an epiphany not about my own MBA, but about certain pillars of my own learning in the past 10 years, especially about the web. What I realized is that there are probably a dozen foundational areas of being an expert on websites, such as web design, web programming, web analytics, business development, product management, email marketing, search engine marketing and organic SEO. What I realized is that you tend to end up an expert in one of these areas, not all. Once you become an expert, you will find that your desire to learn more in that specific field may top out, especially after many years in the field.

This just means you need to get knowledge in the other areas, if you work in the web. Our brains can only handle the same thing day in, day out for just so long. And learning something new does not mean giving up what you know, it means building on what you know by learning a new area, especially if it is related. If your answer is to be happy knowing your little silo of information and that's that, then this kind of person is the perfect company person.

Ford's Assembly Line

If you look at the original concept of Ford's Assembly Line and why it was so ground breaking, it's because of specialization. Each person in the factory would specialize in one small area of making a car. I probably would have quit that job at some point, or maybe I would have moved around the plant and worked on the fenders for a while. I need to get around and learn more about different areas after I master an area of a business. I had for the longest time been considered a web analytics expert. This expertise, which is somewhat uncommon in the market, is in my opinion, not an end unto itself, but one of many disciplines needed to truly understand the web. It is foundational.

The Designer Becomes The Programmer And Vice Versa

I have actually seen web designers start out writing a few PHP programs here and there and turn into a full time programmer. I have seen designers become directors and engineers become writers. We seem to migrate towards not what we know, but what we are good at. In fact, maybe initially we did not even know we were good at these things, but when we found out, by chance, that we were good at it, we decided to like it. I stole that idea from the New York Times article on why Chinese Mothers are superior (They make their kids learn something. They say be good at something, and then one day you will learn to like it!). The Chinese Mother is just a myth I also hear.

Web Education

Let's face it, you can get an education on any subject in 15 minutes today. I use Youtube.com when I cook and watch videos on how to make Indian food. I use Instructables.com to figure out how to do this or that. I research facts that make me as knowledgeable as any doctor, on certain matters, in a matter of minutes. I even used my smartphone while in a retail outlet going out of business recently, the approximate value of a painting on the wall, before it was sold to me. That gave me leverage. We are all starting to do these types of activities. Why? Because it's easy! You probably have your smart-phone right next you right now. We are empowered with the ability to discover and learn at a moment's notice. Think about the impact of this on future generations who will have an answer to any question imaginable in a second. Still the web doesn't give us the core part of an education that we get in the classroom, and that is working in teams, directly with an instructor that can't exactly be mimicked online. The day is coming with Skype, Wifi and iPads where this will not be true anymore…

Great leaders give more than they take!

ON LEADERSHIP

Interestingly enough, the one theme I can find that connects almost every aspect of our lives, childhood, school, work, personal, family is leadership. It may come in many forms with many titles, but it always comes down to responsibility, decision-making and accountability. And trust me; I am not going to give you a diatribe on how great a leader I am, because often I am not. Though, I admit, I aspire to be one. I decided to leaving this article about leadership in this book, because whether you are a start-up or work in a big companies, leadership is still critical to personal success.

Success and leadership are often intermingled, but they are not the same thing. One can be the product of the other, but too often success may come at a cost, sometimes that cost can be leadership-less. That is when success comes at the cost of somebody out there. Greed and avarice is not leadership. In fact financial success is not always leadership and neither is winning always leadership. Though financial success and winning require leadership, but it's an ingredient not the final product. I would classify leadership in its own category. Other words come to mind like ethics and morality. I would not go that far, but these are the underpinnings of leadership.

So I have thrown a lot of words into that conversation. One place I can point to is our childhood. If you are influenced by somebody who embodies leadership it can impact your entire existence. If you were influenced by the opposite of leadership, you may have tendencies to run from taking a position, taking a role in leading or taking control of anything, including your own life.

Quite frankly my tendency is to run from leadership. I know deep inside how much a commitment takes. I finally got married at 42, late in life, because I did not want the commitments involved. But sometimes we are unlikely leaders. Being a parent puts you in a position where you have no choice. You can be a leader of your child and show them the way or you can run. A few people run, I did not. I guess this is a big test in life for all of us.

I have been in charge and will be in charge of all kinds of stuff in my life, including business, personal and sometimes community. And while I don't want the responsibility, I aspire to be the person in charge. In several cases in high school and college I was either the president of an organization or ran my own youth group. I even was in charge of a chunk of a national organization in BBYO. I have owned my consulting company and software business over the years and have had to take responsibility for these companies, meaning paying the bills and making sure the work gets done.

Accountability

There is one place we can all make an improvement in our day to day lives and that is being accountable. It is not always fun. It is not always something we want to do. It means answering a call and talking to a person we don't want to. It may mean for me talking to a client and getting back and having a conversation with someone I quite frankly don't want to talk with. It can mean living up to some level of responsibility in life.

I find the insidious lack of accountability has reared its ugly head in almost every aspect of our lives, mainly because of technology. We used to be able to receive a written or printed letter and write a well written letter back to respond. Back then we had the time to think and write carefully that letter. Today I get almost a hundred emails a day (not including spam, social and promotions), and sometimes I have to log on in the middle of the night to respond to someone, somewhere who needs an answer to a question. It may be something minor. It may be a big issue, but I definitely aspire (once again) to get an answer to that person. Like everybody in some form of technology overload, we end up missing the responses here and there. It comes as no surprise to me, because there is no way a rational person can respond to everything going on. The tweeting and posting on Facebook walls has only increased this to a new level.

The best thing I can do, and you can as well, is to make an effort, figure out what needs to be responded to and what not to respond to.

Real Leaders

I have been around real leaders, and trust me I see things in them I will never have the capability of doing. That's ok. I am more of an observer and supporter than a traditional leader. My leadership skill is based on how I live and not on exactly what I have accomplished. I influence others by how I take actions. We all simply need to look in the mirror and measure ourselves, our capabilities and what we want to get out of life. If you want to succeed and win, especially in business, then learn from existing leadership (the past) and put yourself in situations where the leaders are near you that you can learn from and can influence you, if you are so lucky. This is so critical if you are young and just starting out. The ones who are able to learn from great leaders will go on to be great leaders themselves.

When you are in a start-up you need to not exactly follow the rules; you need to make up the rules.

DON'T BE ORDINARY

As one friend of mine goes back to work after a year or two of being officially unemployed, I offered some words of wisdom, "Don't Be Ordinary".   You can take this to mean many things, because it is a general statement about our condition in life.   You can just do things "the company" way and churn out what is expected of you, or… you can show that you have ideas, that you can communicate and this means you have more to offer the organization that expected as well as our society. We need to show our value more and more, and communicating that value is critical. Of course there are people who like to be ordinary. That's fine. I don't. But that's me. But my reference to Don't Be Ordinary refers to how others view us. My specific advice to an employee going back to work means don't be the person you were (if it was an issue) when you last worked. Be a different person, one who is not looked upon as average. This applies just as well to a person looking at their start-up.

How to be different?

First off there are a tons of ways to be different and less ordinary in our work. There are many ways to start changing. One is to learn to be a better presenter. The info is out there to learn. I personally love Diane Duarte and have read her book *Slide:ology* and a new one *Resonate*. And there is *You Got To Believed To Be Heard* by Bert Decker. My answer is, if you were laid off from a job and told you were not very important or added much to the organization, then change that. Learn to be a great writer and presenter. Each time you are given a chance to communicate, be extraordinary. You can improve your slides, your speaking habits, your dress, your weight, your hygiene, your whatever. We can improve and yes, the little details matter when it comes to being different.

College Rules

I always felt that the whole underlying purpose of college and high school education was to teach us to succeed at following the rules. I quite frankly struggled at this concept.. I was constantly looking for ways to be different yet needing to finish each school class. I was not as interested in competing to be the best, but rather competing to stand-out from the pack. Instead of following the rules exactly, I would always try to find ways around the rules. In fact, I took as many classes where you received education in the field. In both high school and college I was an intern or worked in the field out in the actual real world. I worked on a bunch of political campaigns in high school and eventually worked for Bill Bradley as an intern for college credits. I wrote papers for 6 credits, to not be in class, in both my undergrad and graduate school. I even took a 9 credit summer class where we watched movies all day long and wrote criticisms. To me that was a lot better than studying. When you are in a start-up you need to not follow the rules, you need to make up the rules.

When Different Is Not A Good Thing

My friend Scott Wheeler, who is no longer with us, was a case of person who was different, and not always in a good way. We were close friends and he tried to do the best he could in life. He could not focus at work. He had trouble completing tasks. He was generally a problem in an office setting. I know. Scott worked for me. If you can get up and give an amazing presentation and solve problems, you can change how you are perceived. You do not want to be viewed as a person who thinks differently, but rather one who is thinks in an extraordinary way. But there is a fine line. There are people who are non-conformists and cannot follow any rules. These people should know who they are and where the boundaries exist for them. It is almost like they consistently make bad decisions and don't know when to stop at a red line and don't know when to start moving when the green light changes. That person, yes they are different, troubled, but not really extraordinary. However, that person can easily transform from odd and different to extraordinary, by doing the things in life they are good at. Not everybody is good at a day job. We need to understand our limitations. This is how many of the start-up people end up in a start-up. They could not stand a real job!

Conclusion On How To Be Extraordinary

While working 9 to 5 in an office makes us money (if we have to do it), we are not living in a totalitarian society where we have to do things by the book. And yes, I've been at over 20 years of jobs where we had to do what we are told and do it by the book, so I know that some things you can't change in life. But there is no reason why we can't improve ourselves, read up on giving better presentations, speak better, communicate better. You are often pigeon-holed by organizations as you work your way up the ladder in a big company. This can be good or bad. It is what ultimately lead me to start-ups.

How To Start Again

In the early part of my career I was known as the Garbage Man, because you could throw any task at me and I would get it done. I had to. That was my mantra back then. This is what you have to do sometimes to get ahead if you are starting out. I have had to start over my tech career three times already. You basically go back to step 1 and begin again. Become that garbage man again and get things done.

Differentiating to Succeed

As I learned more about communicating, I realize that you need to differentiate yourself to succeed. And quite often this is not easy to do, since most technical jobs required little or no need to be different. In fact, I just had to meet the basic minimum requirements, do exactly what clients and companies what from me to succeed.

As I had been breaking out of my technology background and growing into management, marketing and roles with branding, speaking, selling, creating product and raising capital, I concluded I needed to be a better communicator. Presentations skills are the first place to start. That is why I went back and finished my MBA. In the end, if you are not starting out, but you want to be in a start-up, you should set a goal of being different and becoming extraordinary. It will serve you well in your first start-up.

Never Lead By Consensus.

CLEAN YOUR TEAM FROM THE TOP DOWN

I rarely clean the our entire refrigerator. Sometimes I will pull a bunch of stuff out and clean a particular row, and sometimes I will go as far as get a sponge out and clean up a little more or so. But one day recently, the refrigerator was looking quite sad and there was all kinds of sap and gook at the bottom, so I decided on the spur of the moment to just start cleaning. Of course at the bottom, if it is real dirty, that is that is the worst part. I got through the entire bottom level, got the entire area white and glossy. That's when I realized, of boy, I should have started cleaning the refrigerator from the top down, not the bottom up. As I would clean the next levels, dirt would run down into the bottom. I thought, wow, this is analogous to fixing technology and technology management in particular.

Start At The Top

If you want to fix a major problem in a Start-Up, a technology company or technology division, you have to start at the top. I am talking about a structural problem. Structural problems can be hard or soft. By hard I mean it is a real technology problem. This can be that the entire division uses outdated technology or bug-filled code. By soft I mean a management issue, where something is wrong and it is a people problem. Often division leaders or executives get together and discuss a problem, and then they of course send out their minions to go fix the problem. Management usually asks others to go and fix the biggest problem, but sometimes that problem is more about leadership than a technical fix. Let's face it, most management are quite frankly the least likely to change, because they are not new or flexible. They are there to get things done, not flex. They have been around a while and their experience can be what got them where they are. But experience quite often can hold them back (we don't know what we don't know). Sometimes to fix a serious problem they have to have the will to change. If they don't they could be technically damaging the company, because very few companies will quickly remove management. They will move people at the bottom around, like middle managers, to try to solve a systemic issue. Making an executive change, that is a difficult task and it impacts the whole organization. Who wants to deal with that.

Rocks Vs. Boulders

Every technology project has its small issues to accomplish and its larger issues. Early on in any project the software is easier to write. As the company, especially an Internet company, gets bigger it becomes more and more difficult to abandon systems for newer ones. Every app or website that has been written becomes obsolete, but most technology people don't want to let go. Why should they? It is what they know!

And Why Change? What would motivate them? That is the issue. What is good for the company, business, or organization is not always what's good for the individual. And I could be wrong about certain situations where the management is terrific and the bottom half is where there is a problem, but honestly the top is where you should first look in solving a hard or soft issue, even in a start-up.

Stay Below The Radar

What all technology people want is for things to go smoothly. Change of course is not easy, so staying out of sight is often the best strategy. So, back to the concept of cleaning from the top of the refrigerator. If you want an entire organization to change their attitude, not only does it have to start at the top, but the top must take their own medicine. It is much easier to lead by doing than by just being a talking head.

Clean Often And Learn

Now, will I ever clean the refrigerator again? Who knows? It seems to get dirty very quickly. Today it is like a brand new refrigerator. Will I get the inertia to do this next time it gets to the point of no return? I can't say? What I can say is next time you look at your refrigerator, if you work in technology, hopefully you will remember this analogy, and instead of working on all these small pieces at the bottom of the technology, you will take a look to start at the top.

Dan Gudema

Thinking Like A Start-Up

Dan Gudema

Web Tech

Most 2 year olds can learn how to use an iPad in less than 10 minutes.

THE NEW WEB TECHNOLOGY WORLD ORDER

Outsource vs. Insource

Over the last couple years I have learned quite a bit about outsourcing to programmers overseas and the IT job market in the US. The two are now totally connected and inter-dependent. And what I am finding is a conundrum. First, the cost of software development has and will continually be driven down by offshore development, some of which I promote. So, you would think there would be less programming jobs and therefor more technology management jobs like web manager, product manager, producer, project manager, Director, VP and CTO. This is especially true when it comes to working with these outsourced teams from the Ukraine and India, for example. Trust me these outsourced teams have moved up to the point where their skill levels are often superior to US based programmers. We thought programming jobs would go away, but what has happened is moving these jobs overseas has just created demand for a whole bunch of new jobs and titles.

More Programming Jobs, Not Less

The truth is, there are even more programming jobs being offered all across the US and less and less management jobs, especially here in South Florida at a time when outsourcing is easy and cuts costs. So what happened? And to be clear, this is just my opinion. Well first off, even when applications are developed overseas and sit on remote websites there still needs to be an accountable local representative who can manage or oversee the deployment of the system. This is the operations person or manager. The biggest drawback to outsourcing is flexibility and communications. You are not in the same room obviously, but Skype makes it seem like we are next to each other. When you have a programmer working with you in the same room (if you were the guy or gal in charge), you are more agile and you are more likely to fix minor things quickly. This is always going to be an issue with outsourcing.

The Heavy Lifting

The biggest positive with outsourcing is the cost and the speed of the heavy lifting. Just think about how you paid a mover when you moved last time. If you moved yourself, it probably took a lot longer to accomplish the task. You I hire a moving company that shows up with 3 big guys who moved it all without any problem. The same thing is true with outsourcing. So when there is some significant application with a lot of technology that needs to be built, sending it overseas totally makes sense, unless you can raise a large sum of capital to keep it all here. But if the system is developed well and costs less, why would you keep it here in the US?

Less Management And Not So Good For MBAs...

But more importantly I see a flattening of IT management across both large companies and SMBs (Small and Medium Businesses), meaning the need and relevancy of levels of people between executives and programmers has declined. So if you are building a building (similar to a big software program), companies, especially smaller companies, they don't see the value in hiring an architect or engineer if you follow the analogy. Smaller and medium sized business owners see the value in the construction worker. In this case the programmer, because programming value is more tangible and measurable than management value, especially during a recession.

Flying Low And Blind

Whether this is a recession issue or not, what this means is 90% of software ventures and technology projects, especially outsourced ones, are often flying blind. You don't always require a project or product manager, but if you are spending more than $50,000 on a software project, you should have a project manager. If your software project has tons of features, unique pricing and other complicated parts then you probably should have a product manager. If you are creating a product for the consumer market, then often you need a quality assurance expert. It sounds logical, but typically only larger companies or funded Start-Ups have these roles, and these roles are declining in the IT profession compared with programmer demand. It tells me that (and I will put on my programmer hat on) that application development has gotten so much better over the years that entrepreneurs and basic users think they can take on these roles and are in fact becoming IT management experts themselves. I have met many of them out there! You would be surprised how many talented individuals have picked up these IT management skills. And some people are great at this, but experience in this area can make all the difference in getting a website or product to market.

Dan Gudema

The beauty of code does not matter. The only thing that matters is the darn thing works well.

PASSWORDS, SECURITY, TECH SNAFU'S & SUPPORT

Well, with a title like "Passwords, Security, Tech Snafu's & Support" I am going to cover in this section a bunch of thoughts on the support process that I have navigated in the past couple years with our speed dating company. This means I may chat about the importance of stability, password security, or issues I have run into trying to keep things running, since there are down times and bugs.

First Things First: What The Heck Have I Gotten Myself Into

Nothing I am saying here is a hard and fast rule. It is based on my experience. Let me first start with the overall situation I am in. Back in 2001 I helped a certain person create a speed dating business. By help, I mean I wrote all the web application code to create a website where people in many, many cities could both run speed dating events and sign up for events. This company, called Pre-Dating, went on to be sold to Cupid.com. When Cupid no longer wanted the business, they sold it back to us. In 2010 I redeveloped the code again from scratch. We recreated the business on a back-end platform called Take It National, i.e. Takeitnational.com. While I did all these things and built all these systems that work (nicely), I still profess that I am by no means an expert or a serious, serious programmer.

1. It Works

The most important rule to me and a lot of top developers I know is that it works and does not crash! This means that my code is not sophisticated, not always in the code hall of fame or MVC perfect or something to write an article or to write home about.

2. No Bugs, But There Is Downtime.

I hate bugs, and of course I work toward no bugs. Who doesn't? There are some down times, but I will get into when that happens and why it will eventually happen. There are a dozen lessons I learned over the last 12 years dealing with these systems, but the fact is you cannot make a perfect system, because even if you made the system perfect, there still would be a crash one day, especially if that is the day the operating system, hardware or the software language gets upgrades.

3. Upgrades, The Bane Of My Existence.

90% of my bugs today are upgrade related. For instance the big one recently was an upgrade to PHP Version 5.4 from 5.2. I found out about it when I got a call from the site manager who told me the site was offline with 404 errors. After a little bit of research reading through the logs, I realized that the errors we were getting were due to an upgrade in PHP. I don't even know when there are upgrades of languages. And why would I think an upgrade would crash my system? So, I found out eventually that this little note on the official PHP site said, hey you had 12 years of us saying this function is going away and to change your code! Wow, that hurt. But I fixed it.

4. Build For The Next Guy.

One thing I have taken into consideration is building a system where another programmer who knows PHP enough can easily take over and work on it. I have even gone as far as keeping code in very specific directories so another programmer could take over and figure it all out.

5. Build Like It Will Be Around A While.

So how would I know that 12 years later, a couple versions of my code would still be running? I didn't. Some guy may have written some mainframe code 30 years ago that is still in production. How would he know that would happen? We don't. Take a few things into consideration. Not doing the most sophisticated ways of doing things helps as well as making sure the code can easily be moved between servers. For instance, we had an application a few years ago that was looking for an E: drive for an extension, this was ASP, and we had just moved the code. There was no E: drive!

6. User Errors

Then there is the case where there looked to be a major error in the system, but the error was caused by user "data" entry. The users had specifically added or changed something that caused the bug. This can happen when you leave back-door admin openings (like text fields with no rules) for administrators to add stuff they are not supposed to. This is why I am becoming more and more negative about HTML content apps on the back-end versus text. With HTML you can mess up the application easily. Most important thing here is to check to see if the problem is user entry created first, before jumping in and programming.

7. The Once In A Lifetime Bug

There is this one bug that happened to me over the years that drove me crazy. A user with an Irish last name, like O'Neil, wanted to make sure their name had an apostrophe in the name. So they tried to force their name through the email signup with an apostrophe. Later on that messes up the application in that it can send a stop code or start code message to the system. So I fixed this. I made it so the users could not enter the apostrophe anymore. Meanwhile a few years later one of my admins gets a call from a customer and then forces the apostrophe into the system via an admin screen.

8. Using System Email Addresses

There is an article that basically says that they got hacked using their company email address vs. using a Google email or large system email address. If a hacker gets control of your mail system, that is where the most damage can occur. How does that happen? They hack into your GoDaddy account and redirect the mail services to their own server. I have read about this happening a few times recently with well documented big cases. And with that, they are able to reset your passwords on sites like Twitter, Facebook even PayPal. How does this mainly happen. Somebody calls your hosting company and tricks them into giving them access to your account. So, there is a real security hole in that the hosting company may let the hacker in. It happens.

So, what I am saying is it is best to use a Gmail or Hotmail email address for the admin accounts, because they will never get control of the back-end of Google. Obviously bad things can happen as well on Google, but it is less likely to lose control of the overall domain.

9. Solve Things Early

General Schwarzkopf had a great saying, (I am misquoting him here, i.e., sic) that "The Quicker You Make A Decision, The Faster You Have Time To Change It". Try to attend to the problem ASAP. So that is why I am always available for a support email, AIM, SMS and make sure the issues are resolved as soon as possible. It may take time to fix things and figure out a problem, but it is important to solve those problems as quickly as we can.

10. You Can't Think Of Everything

I am guilty of many things, and as technology gets more

sophisticated I become guiltier and guiltier as I know less and less. You can't master everything or know everything.

What you can do is learn what does not change so often... things like MS Excel and Linux. In 1989 I went to the book store and there were only 4 or 5 books on computers in local bookstores. Those days ended with thousands of books. And finally today, most of us don't read books, but we can find 10,000+ articles online that help us solve things.

Dan Gudema

80% of web development work is in the planning and 80% of the software development work occurs in the last 20% of the project

WEB MIGRATIONS AND TAKING SITES LIVE

Now let's say you have been brave enough to either hire a web developer or build your own website yourself, or let's say you have been assigned to build out a new website for a large corporation. If you know some PHP/MySQL or have some programming skills, or you are a designer, a "web producer" or web product manager or just a plain old entrepreneur, and you are in the middle of trying to get your website live, I understand your pain.

The Brand New Site

Websites run the gamut. They start from 1-10 page biz card sites, which only show your basic contact us, about us, services, to a full blown combination of existing systems like WordPress & Joomla adding in customized "serious" app development. They can have 10 lines of programming or in the case of one of my projects over 300,000 lines of programming. Either way, a brand new spanking web site with some level of serious programming will have this kind of logarithmic ending to the project. This is even worse than the old 80/20 rule, where 80% of the work is in the last 20%. It's more like 95% of the work occurs in the last 5%.

Why so much work at the end? That's because you typically have a situation where a lot of things are not known till the very end. It does not matter what the developer, project manager, third party guy in India tells you. The hard work in this business starts not on day 1, but day 180, when the petal hits the metal. And this kind of work has more to do with QA than development, and precision, not hand grenade throwing let's kind of get it working. That's why many outsourced websites, to overseas folks, die on the vine or cost 10 times what they projected. This detail work is the work that you, the owner, or a person close to you needs to do. It is not for a guy or gal in a developing nation out there to do. Not to say that overseas development is not cost effective, it's saying that I have my doubts after the 7th inning stretch.

Civil Engineering vs. Web Engineering

Let's compare building a website to the construction process of a building. They are similar in that there should be some type of project plan. Where they differ is that building plans can't change much, once you start building it. The plans for a building are set in stone or the building could collapse and fail. A website is more like a big plumbing project in an old house, even for new websites. You don't know the full extent of the project, sometimes, till you are in the middle of it. That's why many web developers are not so willing to take one price stop shopping when selling their skills. Smarter web developers now realize that the big work can emerge towards the end, if a few big obstacles are discovered.

Digital Feature Discovery

I mention Digital Feature Discovery a lot in my blogs. That's because much of the development process on the web is about discovery. A good case in point is you start building a site, and you end up finding a new opportunity along the way. An example recently for me is we were building this college admissions counseling website and we realized about halfway through the project that there is an opportunity to create a series of pages, when SEO'd that would drive thousands of visitors. We would not have thought of this feature, unless we undertook the project. This is not a sequential process. This is a mind map type of process, where you start and many different directions appear. You have to visualize these directions, and rate them and decide which comes next, which to ignore and which to take on.

The Migration

Ah, the migration. This is when you move a website code and a database from from one server or servers to another. Another way to say this is what a P in the A. When you are moving a website, it is one of those things that can keep you up every night and you are blind while you are doing it.

Even when I had a team of 20 people working for me during a big migration of sites for NTT corp., we could not think of all the details. Our brains cannot think of everything. When I recently migrated Pre-dating.com, one of my projects, I did it myself. This was like saying I am going to move myself, and you have a big house of stuff. It will happen, but it is painful. I have moved to a new home at least 12 times in my adult life. Every time I have to leave something behind. I have to get rid of things I don't want to get rid of. If I don't keep moving, the junk will keep piling up till I move again.

But moving means leaving it.

When migrating, you have this list of all the things that need to happen. Mind you, some techies are great at migrations. But no matter what you know and do, there always seems to be an issue you did not think of. We don't know everything or sometimes we don't know much at all. I moved a site recently and I realized after we moved the site, that the reverse DNS was set up incorrectly. When you looked up the site by IP address it was incorrect. AOL blocked the email. Argh! I got it working, but it was in an area that is not my expertise. I fixed it, like fixing a migraine headache. Another issue on a migration I see all the time is slight differences in the servers. The old server and new server may be the exactly same, but for some reason PHP, MySQL, sql server are not the same. There is always a difference. Hopefully the settings don't cause a major problem, but it often does. I have even seen a migration and 4 months later the real problem appeared out of nowhere. It was always there. We just did not find it. You can't think of everything.

What Am I Saying?

I am just pontificating on the issues involved in taking sites live. I have to give you a big pat on the back when it goes live, whether it's a new site or a migration. This is an accomplishment, regardless of what you techie friends say. There are many sites which refuse to change, move, migrate or improve because of fears of disaster. The disasters, and I have seen them, are going to happen at times no matter what you do. They happen and you deal with it! If you fear the unknown, you may fear it for a reason. Tread lightly when migrating, but pay the price long-term if you don't bite the bullet. The day will come when the site migration is neither planned nor cost effective. It is on that day when you have run out of options. You may lose some of your business or all of it and I have seen it happen. Once you know you have to migrate someday, best to start today. If you have an old web site sitting on an old web server, the time is now to start planning. Trust me, your spanking new start-up service will one day get old. The code will get behind on its release versions. The web will catch up and move you, if you don't migrate first.

By the time you figure out what will happen next with IPTV, it will have a new name and be called something else.

THE END OF CABLE TV AS WE USED TO KNOW IT

In a recent venture I had signed on with, Connect Address, I happened to come upon one aspect of this biz which touched upon IPTV. IPTV stands for Internet Protocol Television. You can do your own research on this, and come to a different conclusion, but essentially IPTV stands for the delivery of television over the Internet. That's a connection like Comcast, Verizon or at&t or Fios or Netflix. We'll get back to Netflix in a moment. In fact one of the issues that surrounds IPTV is what it is not clear what will happen, because quite frankly we are in the middle of the transition to IPTV. Obviously those who control all the cards today, like Comcast, are the established hegemony. There has been an entry into their world at almost every corner from old telcos over Fiber like Fios. There has also been flanking competitors like The Dish Network and DIRECTV.

There Are Competitors, And Then There Are Competitors

The competitors in TV or cable or wireless or whatever you want to call it (because there has been some potential for competitors over electric…), are all after becoming the next form of television delivery. First Youtube and then Hulu and Netflix entered the scene and what you have is a real industry shake-up. So you see a trend. New companies are trying to punch their way through entrance barriers. Recently I noticed that Comcast tossed another 50 HD channels in our direction. Not that I am a lover of Comcast, but this seemed like a nice gesture. What it really was, or is, is a way of throwing us a bone. However, that bone has no meat, literarily. 90% of these so called extra HD channels are copies of the non-HD channels. Even more depressing to me was that 90% of the new channels are either in Spanish or are sports channels. I don't need this! In fact it is too much for me, other than the free Sprout Online (thank you Comcast for one decent channel and late nights that I don't have to keep the kid on my neck).

Comcast's customers are starting to see options on the horizon. This is why Comcast is throwing at customers everything that is cheap and free, in an attempt to keep all its customer happy. It's a temporary fix.

Channel Lineups Are Old School

What I think is going to happen is most of us are going to come to a reality check. Wouldn't you rather have Netflix and basic cable than 200 channels I can't make heads or tails of. The days of a la cart programming are coming! That's what Netflix has been innovating. For me it started with getting a Roku box, the streaming partner of Netflix. You can now get Roku, Netflix and others built in to the TV. Let's just say that Comcast, remarketed as Infinity and some other kind of Netflix mimicry like Comflix. Comcast is trying to keep up with Netflix. Yes, for Comcast there will be a future, but not one where Comcast will necessary control the future. Though Comcast has tons of money and power to try to control the future! However, Comcast's future is not about being the only game in town, but rather the pipe. Their recent acquisition of NBC shows they know this is coming. People will find alternative IPTV channels to watch.

Unique and Amazing Programming

With channels like AMC, FX, HBO, ShowTime and even now Netflix offering original programming I think the future will be quite different. Let's just say that Youtube and Hulu I expect will have original shows and movies, just like Netflix the others offering programming.

What does this mean? Well, for one many of us will want to buy that content, even if it is $2-$7 on the fly. Do we all need 200 channels and tons of fluff. No. With IPTV I expect more pay for play, more mini subscriptions or low end Netflix like $9 a month services. A la carte sounds best to me and what I really think will make some future player a bundle. Get in, get out. The days of locking us into month after month contracts may have been good for the past, but those days are numbered. Amazon and Apple will one day produce a TV show and original programming. Trust me, it's coming.

Wi-Fi Built In TVs... The Apocalypse Is Upon Us

On a side note, my wife has become quite obsessed for looking for Wi-Fi built in TVs (ever since I smashed one of our 6 TVs). The key to Wi-Fi built in is the ability to have the TV automatically online and the ability to easily surf to an independent online channel and run IPTV as you see fit. Yes, you still have to pay a Comcast or a Verizon (or steal the local Starbucks Wi-Fi), but what you end up with is a way to get to independent programming or whatever you want. The Roku box we got from Netflix started with like 5 channels, Pandora and some crap, but eventually about 40 churches, gaming channels, music and even a Roxstar app that allowed my wife to push her DVDs into the cloud and access them through Roku became available. Eventually she found Plex, an even better way to manage your content locally not through the cloud! All tons of great stuff, but not until your TV is connected is any of this possible. The built in Wi-Fi is only on very few TVs we found. None at Costco or Wal-mart, yet. My prediction was that 2 years from today they ALL will be Wi-Fi enabled. And now they are! Lookout Comcast, the last days are here and things will never be the same after that. But don't fret Comcast, you will do even better, because we all need more bandwidth... tons more. And you ask why. See below, the future.

The Inevitable IPTV Future

So as IPTV creeps and crawls into our lives, we will one day wake up and say, damn, how did everything get IP based (that means over the Internet). It's simple. It's not just a trend. It's a reality. And I see a hell of lot more going on down that pipe, extending the internet to places, it quite frankly does not belong, but it's going there. For instance, I foresee on our TVs the complete merging of Internet sites and video, creating a whole new level of reality IPTV, where you participate in the channel locally. Ah, there will be webcams and there will be video calls over the TV. Will it be Skype, who knows? But let's just say you are watching a football game and want to make a call and interact with your friends (video phone) as they all watch the game together. That's a spot I am quite interested in, because of Connect Address. Let's just say you are watching a new wave of game shows in which millions participate along with the live show using IPTV. That's where it's going, and it really opens up Internet interactivity in ways that have not yet been thought of. Trust me your spanking new product or service will one day get old and the web will catch up and move past you. You need to stay ahead of the curve and pay attention to the trends.

Techo-garble

ON WORDS: WEB LINGUISTICS

People ask me questions about this piece of technology and that piece of technology. What I am often asked, even by experts themselves, is whether this is the right term or that is the right term to explain a particular technology. Technology wording is changing every day. And quite often usage of wording is necessary for a technology discussion or a pitch to raise capital. You need to get the wording correct to be considered competent. Either way, there is some confusion about the difference or use of the words in technology today. An example would be a Plugin vs. an Add-on vs. Extension.

I am putting together a list of used and miss-used words that I am hearing a lot of in Internet ventures, from Angels, VCs and just kids playing with web sites. These words have become interchangeable within each group, mainly because the general population really does not see a difference, but in the know VCs and tech people know there is a difference.

I know I will embarrass myself here because there are sticklers who are more specific about these words and their use. I am just pointing out the blurring of the lines and how the web has changed the language and meaning of these words for users, who find themselves having to explain things to people on calls to their technology providers, whether it's the phone company, cable or third party provider. And if you are pitching a start-up, you need to get these words correct!

Words have a funny way of changing over the years. I am writing this blog entry as would William Safire in the New York Times Sunday addition I used to read as a kid. He would cover all the new words he has heard and give a history to where they came from in their origin often citing the Oxford Dictionary. I read it every week carefully as a kind. I won't go as far as the Oxford dictionary, but I will discuss these words in a way that is helpful if you are going to pitch for capital amongst experienced technology professionals.

Plugin, Add-on, Extension

All three words seem to convey the same existential meaning, a piece of a software that creates new value that can be added or not added to your existing piece of software. This is not the same as an App. These are extra stuff. I am sure they had historic meanings for each and when they first came into use. And of course WordPress uses Plugin and Joomla uses Add-ons. Quite honestly these 3 are becoming completely interchangeable. If you are giving a start-up pitch I think Plugin is the best word for this.

Feature, Function

Somewhere along the way, while programmers know technically what a function is, the actual user does understand the difference between features and functions that occur when you add-on something new to software. They just see a new piece of working software that accomplishes something for them, like a sitemap plugin! For end users feature and function are synonymous, though programmers would beg to differ. Proper use for a start-up pitch if you are talking about how the product works is Feature.

Widget, Drop-in

Once again thank WordPress for using the ubiquitous word Widget, which is a little different than a Feature. These are things that you put in your software yourself and they go to work. There are occasionally drop-in apps that work like a widget. The widget reference I think is different than other extension type applications, in that it is specific to a place on the page. And a widget can be dropped into an existing app if it supports widgets.

Pop-up, Pop-Under, Light-box, Hover

These are things that just annoy us that show up when we arrive or leave a website or mobile app. I am including a Light-box here, because that is a thingy that takes over your screen with a dark silhouette in the background. You typically need to click an X in order to get rid of the Light-box. The Light-box is a pop-up of sorts, but it uses a local function, so it is technically not a pop-up. A hover, as you know comes up with a mouse on-over. These 4 words have kind of merged into one thing for users, extra things or functionality that occurs on an action by a user. But users like everything else don't always get the difference.

Template, Theme, Skin, Brand

What has happened with these four words is they have come to virtually mean the same thing to people, whereby the look and feel or Brand of the software can change, yet the guts or application remains the same. Everybody talks about where to get their newest theme, like my favorite ThemeForest.com. Yet, we know as programmers that a template is more than just a visual these days. What has happened in WordPress is Themes have programming in them. So the lines are getting blurred.

Program, Application, Platform, System, App

Most of these are old technology words. That have various technical meaning to programmers, yet to the user, there is no difference. These words refer to the computer program. Even the word App has now on its own come out and stands for specifically a Mobile or Smartphone app. The word Platform for PHP and .Net programmers has come to mean which method they are using to program... Not important to end users though.

Smartphone, Tablet, iPad, iPhone, Mobile, Cellular, Cell

Even I, having worked for a cellular phone company for 10 years at one point, see the words merging here. We know there is a difference between Tablet and Smartphone, but have you really looked closely at the Ipad Mini, the iPhone 6, the Samsung Note or the Galaxy S4. What is happening is all these words refer to some type of nice UI device you can carry around and get to your stuff, surf the web, make a call, etc. Does it really matter in the end what you call it all, as long as it provides what you are looking for. If you want to sum it all up for your start-up pitch, I would use Smart Device.

Cloud, Hosting

I have myself been guilty of merging these 2 words of late. The word cloud has come to mean, in my eyes, now pretty much all hosting. I am completely technically wrong, but am I theoretically wrong? Not sure. I have put down cloud on a couple VC pitches recently and I am just waiting for somebody to challenge me. They haven't. They get it. Cloud is inclusive of hosting (in my eyes). You can argue with me if you want here!

MVP, Beta

Everybody uses Most Viable Product (MVP) in the Start-Up world today. The fact that it sounds like an Baseball MVP or Most Valuable Player, is why I love this word. It is used to describe the most minimum product you can produce to get your product to market. For Start-Up guys it represents getting to market, plain and simple. If you have an MVP you are live. Beta refers, in today's web/app lingo, as a site which is just about live but still has some bugs. It means the app/site has not been released to the general public. There have been some arguments among partners over whether to say Beta or not. The marketing guys never want to say or admit Beta. The tech guys like me want to be honest with the world and just tell them it is new and can break! Seems like things change over time. For instance, being in Beta has become a cool thing recently. You can some belief that the site is new and fresh, and you may be one of the few who have tried it. That is a psychology point that is now truer than it has been in the past. If you are giving a start-up pitch I would use MVP. It's in vogue right now.

I probably missed a few words here. Hopefully you get the overall drift of these words. They have meaning for everybody in several ways, yet they are merging in meaning overall. Within the programming world, you have specific conventions, but in the outside world of everyday people, they are just terms we use to help us communicate, so what if accidentally call your Nexus an iPhone? You will just nod your head, and say "yes", you meant my iPhone? If you are giving a start-up pitch, take your time and get this right. You may have considered calling it one thing, when investors thing it is another.

Thinking Like A Start-Up

A FEW FINAL WORDS

If you have gotten this far and are finishing up reading Thinking Like A Start-Up, that means I have held your attention long enough in this crazy over-connected world to get a few points across here and there. If you have simply flipped to the back of the book and are reading for the first time that is ok. That is how we sometimes process information. If you need to work your way backwards that is ok as well. In Thinking Like A Start-Up I have tried to cover the gamut of Internet business, web technology, online marketing and people issues you go through in order to develop websites and mobile applications. This is not a guide book. It is just a bunch of thoughts about Start-Ups and web tech projects in general. There is a lot of learning involved in the process. I believe that we are just at the infancy of Internet technology with new 3D, wearable technology and other new types of technology that are making it possible to Start-Up and capture market share. The trick is figuring out the next trend. Remember, tech trends are a train. The train can be coming down the track. The train could be passing us by right now. The train can be long gone from the station. You need to decide which train to catch if you are going to succeed. This book is hopefully the first in a series of books I intend on writing about Tech Start-Ups. Please buy the next in the series. Thank You. Dan Gudema

Thinking Like A Start-Up

YOUR READING LIST

Through this book I mention some of my favorite tech related start-up books. This is your reading list. If you are a tech start-up and have not read these book, you need to start now!

Get Real: The Smarter, Faster, Easier Way to Build a Successful Web Application by Jason Fried, David Heinemeier Hansson and Matthew Linderman
Rework by Jason Fried, David Heinemeier Hansson
The Art of The Start by Guy Kawasaki
Reality Check by Guy Kawasaki
Rules For Revolutionaries by Guy Kawasaki
Don't Make Me Think by Steve Krug
Do More, Faster by Brad Feld
World Famous by David Tyreman
The Wisdom Of Crowds by James Surowiecki
What the Dog Saw by Malcom Gladwell
Outliers by Malcom Gladwell
The Launch Pad by Randall Stross
The Lean Startup by Eric Ries
All Marketers Are Liars by Seth Godin
Wikinomics by Don Tapscott and Anthony D. Williams
Getting Into Your Customer's Head by Kevin Davis
SLIDE:OLOGY by Diane Duarte
Resonate by Diane Duarte
You Got To Believed To Be Heard by Bert Decker
Inevitable Surprises by Peter Schwartz

Thinking Like A Start-Up

ABOUT THE AUTHOR

Though Dan Gudema aspired to be a writer as a kid, he was never able to fulfill that journey up till now. Dan has worked as a software developer, corporate manager, entrepreneur and consultant. Dan is a fixture in the tech Start-Up community in South Florida. Dan has worked as an IT and Web manager or consultant for a variety of corporations like Bell Atlantic Mobile, abc distributing and NTT/Verio. In 2001 Dan co-founded and developed as a programmer Pre-Dating Speed Dating, which became the largest speed dating company in the US. It was sold to Cupid.com in 2004. In 2014 Dan became a co-founder of Krowde, a new kind of private mobile social network. Dan is also a partner in DSX Labs, a tech incubator in Boca Raton, FL, where he regularly meets with Internet and Mobile Start-Ups. Originally from Parsippany, NJ, Dan moved to South Florida in 1997. Dan attended the University of Maryland for his BA and has an MBA from Florida Atlantic University.

www.ingramcontent.com/pod-product-compliance
Lightning Source LLC
Chambersburg PA
CBHW030928180526
45163CB00002B/502